LEGENDS & LORE OF THE OLD SOUTHWEST

JESSICA LAUGHLIN

Published by The History Press
An imprint of Arcadia Publishing
Charleston, SC
www.historypress.com

First published 2025

Manufactured in the United States

ISBN 9781467170130

Library of Congress Control Number: 2025944912

Notice: The information in this book is true and complete to the best of our knowledge. It is offered without guarantee on the part of the author or The History Press. The author and The History Press disclaim all liability in connection with the use of this book.

For my husband, Chad.
The one by my side on the journeys through timeless mountains, rivers, and deserts.

CONTENTS

ACKNOWLEDGEMENTS

Crow of the Southwest. *Jessica Laughlin.*

This book is an accumulation of my love for western history, art, and travel. My greatest inspiration for the writing and illustrations came from the people of the past, who made the Southwest into a vibrant region of blended histories and cultures.

My husband, Chad, and I, along with our sweet dog, Gracie, have traveled many miles together. The memories of our journeys on the road are woven into the pages of this book. A special thank-you to my grandmother Betty Stone for all of the fun we've had together and everything she taught me. Thank you to my dear family and friends—Leslie, Dan, Darren, Taren, Bethany, Danielle, and Lindsey. In loving memory of my grandfather Orval, Sheri, Linda, Anita, and Dale.

I would like to especially share my gratitude for my acquisitions editor, Laurie Krill. Her belief in this book from the beginning, as well as her talent in editing and encouragement, has meant so much to me. I'm forever grateful to the team at Arcadia Publishing and The History Press and to my senior editor, Ryan Finn, for all of their contributions to the publication of this book. It's been an honor and a dream to tell the story of the legendary Southwest.

PART I
NEW MEXICO

Doña Tules and the Notorious Burro Alley

In the early days, before New Mexico was a state, it was a territory and part of Mexico under the control of Spain beginning in 1610. Nearly two hundred years later, Mexico became a country of its own in 1821, after the Mexican War of Independence. At the time, the boundary of the United States went only as far west as Missouri. One of the first trails to cut into this new frontier was the Santa Fe Trail, which officially opened in 1821, coinciding with Mexican independence. This trail created new trading opportunities between merchants from the United States, Mexico, and Indigenous communities. Along with Anglo-Americans moving into the area, Mexicans were also moving north for the dream of prosperity.

During this turbulent time of transition after the war, a young Maria Gertrudis Barceló migrated north with her family from Sonora into the new territory, "Nuevo México," now under Mexican control. They settled in Tome, a rural town south of Albuquerque. Growing up against the conditions of war and poverty affected Barceló's desire to achieve more, and it also gave her a fighting spirit. Determined to succeed, she learned to read and write, which was uncommon among her peers. In her downtime, she played cards and especially liked the three-card game of monte. Admirers sought to win her affection as a teenager, but she waited until she was twenty-three to wed Manuel Sisneros, who was a few years younger than herself. Most women took the last names of their husbands, but Barceló chose to retain her sense

Doña Tules. *Jessica Laughlin.*

of independence by keeping her maiden name. They had two sons together, but both died shortly after their births. Loss weighing on them, the couple eventually adopted two girls.

The pair decided to move to Santa Fe around 1825, where the small town was growing rapidly due to the influx of newcomers off the Santa Fe Trail. When they first arrived, they operated a small gambling venue illegally on the outskirts of town. Their clientele primarily included traders, mountain men, and travelers passing through. Barceló had a grander vision though and wanted to establish herself in a location where she could make a fortune using the same strategy on wealthier men. Somewhere along the line, she was given the nickname Doña Tules. "Doña" was a Spanish title given to women who were held in high regard, and *tules* translates to a type of delicate fabric, frequently used in lace, formal dresses, and veils—a fine lady in lace. Little is known of her husband's involvement in her business endeavors, and he seems to fall off the historical records due to her retaining property titles, along with other investments, in her name alone.

During Santa Fe's booming years, the plaza's square would be swarming with livestock and rushing with trade each day. Animals, furs, blankets, and other items were bartered. Currencies of various kinds were exchanged and language barriers broken. A collaboration between men and women of these differing cultures took form. These multicultural roots of Santa Fe trace back to this era during the mid-nineteenth century. Taking a chance on fate, Doña Tules made her mark on the scene at this time in 1835. Spending her own money, she purchased a spacious brick building just off the plaza, where the price of property was reasonable due to its less obvious location on an alleyway. Not only was it off the beaten path, but this lane was also dubbed "Burro Alley," for it was where firewood was sold off the backs of burros.

Wise beyond her years, she recognized the need to turn the interior into a luxurious space to counter the location. For starters, dirt or wood floors would not do the trick. Her casino would be carpeted instead, with candlelit chandeliers and other unusual elements from America's East Coast lining the walls. This exuded a sense of class, despite being a gambling hall and brothel. A perfect combination of sophistication, blending with the seedier side of life, was a welcome change in this wild frontier. Every walk of life was appreciated in her casino, as long as they had the ability to play. The atmosphere drew in not only travelers but also locals for a good time. Soon, even men of Santa Fe's prominent society were curious enough to visit her establishment and became loyal clients. Her plan worked.

Everything about Doña Tules was a contradiction—a madam and gambler who wore a crucifix of gold around her neck. On the one hand, she enjoyed drinking and smoked cigars, but on the other, she held herself gracefully as the most respectable of ladies. And although her features were soft, she was never to be disrespected. She encouraged her patrons to fully enjoy themselves as they lost large sums at her monte table. She wore femininity like a soldier wears armor, and she used her mature beauty to her benefit. She could make a losing man feel special, even if he lost while being taken in by her spell. Concealed under layers of lace, she was the same little girl who wanted more than poverty, hustling every moment of the day and night to achieve better for herself. She never forgot the struggle of her youth and was a charitable woman to those less fortunate, earning her favor even among priests.

Burro Alley in Santa Fe. *Jessica Laughlin.*

Burro Alley was where Santa Fe's diverse society all converged. Spanish guitar and laughter echoed down the lane. Lively banter of Spanish and English blended as one. Intoxicated men sauntered in and out among the burros. Their mood depended on whether they had lost or won. Young women bared their shoulders as they made their rounds, with lips of bright red to mask their desperation. On this alley, a man could leave it all behind, regardless of the social status that he wore during the day. There was simply no place like it in town that had the same ambiance, and because of this, her power grew, as did her clientele. After all, knowing how to play the game in more ways than one was her best advantage.

Alongside her gaming revenue, she invested in real estate and other ventures. This was exceptionally enterprising when considering women in the mid-1800s had very few rights, if any, apart from their husbands. One can imagine all eyes on her as she sauntered down the street, dressed in high fashion, with her hair styled on her head as a queen wears a crown. While townspeople must have considered her immoral, they couldn't refute that her rejection of a woman's traditional place in society had oddly earned her profound respect among men. Whether they wanted to admit it, those

Santa Fe Plaza in the summer. *Denver Public Library Special Collections.*

who shamed her likely wished they emitted that same confidence. While she was untraditional in her way of life, she somehow managed to provide her daughters with everything that she could only have dreamed of having herself. So perhaps the judgments from others eluded her, rolling off her back onto the dusty ground.

The Mexican-American War broke out in 1846. Rather than side with the Mexicans, her native countrymen, she did the opposite of what one might have expected. She assisted the Americans with intelligence and proved to be helpful in their occupation of the territory. Perhaps, as with cards, she already knew what the winning hand would be, and therefore it was wiser to side with the more powerful of the two armies. She hosted American soldiers at her hotel and casino, treated them with the utmost respect, and became well acquainted with General Stephen Kearny. After the Americans won the war and took control of Santa Fe, she attended a ball at the La Fonda on the plaza, gracing the arm of the general himself.

She was a woman of her own, notorious and seductive. Throughout tales of Santa Fe, her name still remains, as does Burro Alley. Her petite stature took a bold stance against the heavy weight of men. And while she may not have been the image of holiness, she ironically was buried among the saints within the La Parroquia Chapel, now the Cathedral Basilica of St. Francis of Assisi. Her funeral was as lavish as the world she invented for herself. A world that could only have happened once, during a fragile turning of time, in old Nuevo México.

The Taos Pueblo and Art Colony

Few places feel as authentic as the High Road to Taos. This fabled road, woven like a snake through the remote New Mexico landscape, begins north of Santa Fe, gradually climbing into the Sangre de Cristo Mountains. It calls to dreamers and wanderers, or those looking to get off the grid. Rather than the highway hustle, with familiar fast-food chains and gas stations at every stop, byways like this one peer into a time before modern convenience. For travelers, this may feel different, but to longtime residents, it's been a way of life for generations. Time doesn't race by in Taos, but instead flows as gently as the Rio Grande.

Along the route, adobe structures blend quietly into the scenery, basking in the golden sun on clear afternoons. Their raw essence is everything that

Taos Pueblo. *Jessica Laughlin.*

goes against our industrial and urbanized world, but nevertheless adobe stands proud in its defiance. Perhaps this is why so many artists have been drawn to the region. Famed artists and writers of the twentieth century like Georgia O'Keeffe, Maynard Dixon, Ansel Adams, and D.H. Lawrence were forever changed by their first venture to Taos.

Landscape painters Ernest Blumenschein and Bert Phillips were two of the original Anglo artists to arrive in Taos in 1898 when their wagon wheel broke on a trip to Mexico from Denver. The nearest town happened to be Taos. After their wheel was repaired, they could have been on their way, but something about the enigmatic terrain compelled them to stay. If it hadn't been for the setback on their journey, the art scene of the Southwest may never have moved forward. Around 1915, Taos started to find its way onto the map as an art colony, due to the establishment of the Taos Society of Artists, which included Blumenschein and Phillips as two of the six founding members.

This relation to the creative reached beyond Taos as their works began to appear in New York City galleries. For those living in the cities, paintings and photographs of this unusual part of the country, rich in rusty hues and native life, provided a striking contrast to their own reality. These pieces of art gave their viewers a faraway place to imagine. The allure of the Southwest only deepened in collective consciousness as more art emerged from this strange location. Along with visual artists came writers and other bohemians. While

Artist in Taos, New Mexico. *George L. Beam, Denver Public Library Special Collections.*

they certainly made Taos famous, the area's Indigenous people had called Taos home for well over a millennium.

Ascending beyond deserts, into valleys of low hills and pinyon pine, relics of old Spain dot the countryside. Influence of Spanish colonization is highlighted in the churches and missions punctuating the horizon. These places of religious and cultural significance generally have remained unaltered for more than two hundred years. Some of the churches still serve as centerpieces of their communities, such as San José de Gracia in Las Trampas or San Antonio de Padua in Cordova. While remarkable in their histories, their presence on the landscape is a mere fraction of time compared to that of the Taos Pueblo.

Taos Pueblo, located north of the town of Taos, is by far New Mexico's most iconic landmark. It's been photographed and painted more than any other structure in the Southwest. Believed to be constructed around AD 1325, its longevity makes it an anomaly. For one thing, the mere survival of such a pueblo illustrates the ingenuity of the original inhabitants, who used only a mixture of water, straw, and earth to form the adobe clay. Not only is it architecturally a masterpiece, but it's also hailed as the longest continuously inhabited pueblo in America.

Much like the Rio Pueblo de Taos River, bloodlines flow through this land as pure as water. For centuries, families passed their property rights on to their children. Each generation wore their heritage with pride and maintained the pueblo. Many Tiwa now live in more modern housing nearby. However, there are some full-time residents residing within the pueblo, foregoing running water and electricity. Where most Native tribes were nomadic or forced off their homelands, the Tiwa managed to hold on to their property against all odds. The pueblo structures are owned solely by decedents of original ancestors. The freedom and rightful ownership enjoyed by the tribe in present times took centuries of struggle to attain.

Taos Pueblo was constantly threatened by invading factors beyond their control. One of the most consequential encounters was the arrival of Spanish conquistadors in 1540, led by Francisco Vázquez de Coronado, during an expedition to find a rumored "Seven Cities of Gold." His troops were often violent and exploited Natives. The Tiwa were no exception. After two years, his expedition was considered a failure by the Spanish government, and he retreated to Mexico without having found gold. He had discovered land that could be conquered, though, and this planted a seed in the Spanish

View of Taos Pueblo. *O.T. Davis, 1926, Denver Public Library Special Collections.*

Taos children. *Edward S. Curtis, circa 1905, Library of Congress.*

empire that grew wildly for years to come. Although the Tiwa resisted, by the early 1600s they were living under Spanish rule. A mission was erected, and to remain in their cherished pueblo, they were required to convert to Catholicism. As a tenacious people, they did what was necessary to survive. Wars and tyranny were an ever-present burden they faced to hold on to this small piece of earth.

In the soul of every person is the desire to be free of the shackles of oppression. For decades the Tiwa lived under a regime whose customs were wholly different from their own. When Mexico gained independence from Spain in 1821 after a raging and lengthy war, Taos Pueblo also experienced a sense of liberation. The Mexicans denounced the cruel treatment of Indians and role the missions played in converting their beliefs. After the war, they were finally able to return to their Native culture, but this would be challenged once again in 1846 during the Mexican-American War.

With this history in mind, it's no surprise that the threat of impending control was the catalyst of the Taos Revolt. The encroachment by the United States on what was at that point legally Mexican land was met with distain. Hispanics and Indigenous people of the region had formed alliances and lived harmoniously under Mexican rule for more than twenty years since defeating Spain. They knew well the impending consequences of newly elected President James K. Polk's vision of Manifest Destiny. One of Polk's primary goals was to extend U.S. power to the farthest reaches of the West. Occupancy of the territory had already begun, and they couldn't trust their future to a new government. The looming threat of invasion was intensely feared. Even if it meant risking their families and land, they chose to defend their own.

Around fires in the night, they gathered and planned to wage war against several U.S. officials living in the village of Taos. Their target was the first territorial governor, Charles Bent, who had long resided in the village as a fur trader and mountain man. He also helped build Bent's Fort on the Santa Fe Trail alongside his brother, William. The fort provided critical supplies to pioneers and was also an important trading partner to tribes of the plains. The knowledge he obtained of the area's intricate dynamics led to his eventual role in government. Much like his brother-in-law, Kit Carson, men involved in the fur trade were valuable to the U.S. mission of westward expansion. They understood geography of the West, often spoke Native languages, and were familiar with the area's tribes.

Bent wasn't expecting anything out of the ordinary when he awoke to his last day on that cold January morning in 1847. It had been merely four months since he was appointed as governor. Without warning, a substantial group of Mexican and Tiwa men forcibly entered his home shortly after he arose from bed. He had no hope of survival, as he was attacked, shot, and scalped. His wife and children were unharmed, but they witnessed the brutality. The United States retaliated at the San Geronimo mission in Taos Pueblo, where men, women, and children sought refuge from the counterattack. Similar to a fort, the mission was difficult to infiltrate, even with cannons. This led the army to set the building ablaze, and it's contended that around 150 souls perished in the fire.

The concept of right and wrong in history is a complex notion. It's easier to peer into the past with judgment. Yet like the adobe walls containing all the histories of this towering pueblo, the truth is muddy and blended over time in the layers applied by those who came before us. Even into the mid-twentieth century, the rights of the Tiwa continued to be tested. However, they were no longer alone in their struggle. Artists, writers, and photographers became their advocates. Their fame and voices assisted the tribe in fighting against further attempts to acquire their land. In 1970, they also assisted in persuading President Richard Nixon to return forty-eight

A Taos woman outdoors at Taos Pueblo. *Horace S. Poley, 1895, Denver Public Library Special Collections.*

A Taos man on a horse at Taos Pueblo. *George L. Beam, Denver Public Library Special Collections.*

A Taos man painting on a canvas at Taos Pueblo. *George L. Beam, Denver Public Library Special Collections.*

thousand acres of national forest to Taos Pueblo. The Tiwa's sacred Blue Lake was included in the transfer.

Beginning with a broken wagon wheel on the outskirts of town, an unlikely bond formed between the Tiwa and the community of artists. Their relationship grew from a place of mutual respect, as both groups held common ideals about life and an appreciation of Taos. The magic that seemed to lure the artists here had purpose beyond their art. In sharing a vibrant culture with the nation through their creativity, they provided a better understanding for its need to be protected. Alongside the Tiwa, they helped guard the freedom and lands for generations to follow.

The Taos Hum

Taos is a mystical place, where spiritual awakenings are common. Whether it's because of the scenery, culture, or art, people gravitate to the region for the experience. However, it's something auditory in nature that seems to be the real mystery. The "Taos Hum" has often been described as a low vibration, rumbling, or humming sound, and not of the pleasing kind. Some individuals claim that it drove them to the brink of insanity in searching for a solution. Fortunately, only a small percentage of the population in Taos hears the hum, but those who do are certain of its presence. This constant companion of the "hearers" has even stunned scientists. It's been the subject of scientific investigations, and although theories emerged, none was ever solidified or proven. Because only some people hear the sound, it draws skepticism from those who can't, but the extensive list of reports is undeniable. The wide variety of people it affects also suggests that the hum doesn't favor any particular group.

It should be noted that those who truly experience the hum oftentimes feel cursed by its infiltration into their life. Taos residents complained that the hum's possible connection to a source of government activity at Los Alamos drew the attention of New Mexico Congressional delegates, who subsequently sent a research team to investigate in 1993. The team included scientists from the University of New Mexico, Los Alamos National Laboratory, Phillips Air Force Laboratory, and Sandia National Laboratories. Throughout the study, they utilized advanced microphones and measured seismic activity and electromagnetic fields. Their research attempted to find the source and alleviate concern, but their reports were inconclusive.

Even though the Taos Hum first received wide attention due to this report, there have been forms of a hum described around Taos in prior decades. In 1917, art patron and writer Mabel Dodge Luhan described the scenic mesas: "It was intensely silent out there without the stirring of anything. And yet, I seem to hear inside the silence, a high continuous humming, like a song, and it made me happy." Was this only a poetic interpretation, or did she hear a hum? In this account, the sound she heard was defined as a pleasant tone.

The serenity found in the area has been written about for well over a century, but this differs from the fierce geology that created the stunning mesas and mountains. When looking at it from a geologic perspective, Taos is located within a highly active area of the Rio Grande Rift, a fracture in the earth caused by tectonic shifts tracing back millions of years. This is visually apparent when driving over the dramatic Rio Grande Gorge Bridge, northwest of Taos, which extends across a deep chasm roughly six hundred feet above the river. The river follows the path of the rift, and to each side, mesas reach for miles until they hit the base of mountains. Faults throughout the rift continue to emit insignificant yet frequent tremors. Some claim that the humming sound could be related to this geologic force—only heard by those sensitive enough to the vibrations.

Whether the Taos Hum is of man-made or natural origins, it's a phenomenon that evokes various opinions and conspiracies. Throughout the world, other unusual hums have been reported, but investigations of this kind are difficult to prove. In particular, the Taos Hum is one of the most theorized and debated of its kind. We may never know why it selects only certain people. For those unable to hear the hum, it's an oddity that continues to fascinate, as all infinite mysteries do.

"Black Jack" Ketchum and the Restless Town of Clayton

Clayton is a remote town in northeastern New Mexico, over the line from West Texas and the Oklahoma Panhandle. It sits within a desolate stretch of flat-mixed prairie, where remnants of old wagon wheels lay rotting on the plains here and there. This was cattle country in the 1800s and also the site of the most gruesome hanging in the state's history. At one point, Clayton seemed destined to grow with the arrival of the railroad, but optimism took a turn because of this macabre event and the mood was

The train robbery. *Jessica Laughlin.*

never the same. It was all because of one infamous man who went by the name Black Jack Ketchum.

In every outlaw's story there's some good mixed in with the bad. There's also a certain point where they take a turn toward darkness, becoming criminals. Once they embark on a life of crime, they can never go back. Thomas Ketchum was born on Halloween in 1863. His father had a career as a coroner prior to relocating his family from Illinois to the unsettled country of central Texas near the San Saba River. When Tom was merely five years old, his father passed away, leaving his blind mother a widow raising several children. She followed him to the grave in 1873. The effects of this trauma must have destroyed his innocence. Losing two parents at a pivotal stage in his development left him scarred, but he covered his grief with a tough outer shell.

His eldest brother, Green, went into cattle ranching, taking a ten-year-old Tom under his wing, along with his other brother Sam. They worked for him as cattle hands for several years and were raised around the culture of cowboying. By the time Tom was twenty-seven, he had grown bored of the same flat horizon and left for New Mexico sometime around 1890. A few years later, when Sam was down on his luck in Texas, he also took off for New Mexico to join Tom. Green, however, remained behind, where he became successful in ranching. Whether intentional or not, losing touch with his brothers after their departure from Texas was probably the best decision he made. After all, once Tom and Sam were together again, they drifted from town to town, robbing individuals and businesses. They relied on their charisma and good looks as they gallivanted around the saloons, evading repercussions by staying on the move. Rough frontier towns like Cimarron and Las Vegas, New Mexico, were frequent stops where they lavishly spent their stolen cash.

During their heyday of violent robberies, they also ventured into Arizona and Colorado, meeting other like-minded outlaws who began to ride with them as a gang. They were even known at times to ride among Butch Cassidy's Wild Bunch. On the trail, Tom earned the nickname "Black Jack." The gang's hard lifestyle and petty crimes soon no longer satisfied their quest for wealth, and consequently they began to think of larger prospects. Trains seemed like an easy target. They were now the preferred method of transporting goods and passengers across the country, but in certain places, desolate stretches made trains vulnerable to robberies. An especially vulnerable piece of track was in the northern region of New Mexico. Because the conductor didn't have a means of communication between stops, it was easier for a heist to take place. The outlaws could get off with whatever they had stolen long before the conductor contacted law enforcement. Although they robbed passenger trains by gunpoint, they preferred raiding mail cars, which contained more valuables and warranted less risk to their own lives.

After a robbery, the gang couldn't just take their cash, gold, and jewels to a bank. They would instead hide it where only they knew the location, with a plan to eventually gather their hidden fortune. It's possible that they thought the train robberies would supply them with enough to live comfortably and that this part of their lives would drift into smoky memories. But once an outlaw always an outlaw, and maybe they just enjoyed the thrill of it all. Their youth, wrought with turmoil and boredom, receded further into the past. Tending to cattle on the ranches of Texas was a far cry away from this life of women, drinking, and gambling—all of which came easy to the brothers.

Although they were close, like any siblings, they had their share of disagreements. As hot-tempered as these two were, their last moments together were likely hostile. The reason they fell apart remains unknown. Along with a posse from the gang, Sam coordinated his last train robbery without Black Jack in July 1899. He chose the Colorado Southern train, which was en route to its destination through Folsom, New Mexico. The robbery went as anticipated. Just when they thought they were out of dodge, a team of lawmen hunted them down, finding the thieves hiding in a cave near Turkey Creek Canyon just outside Cimarron. A violent gunfight ensued. Sam was shot in the left arm; the sheriff and several deputies were killed. Managing to escape the scene bloodied and wounded, Sam was later caught and brought immediately to the Santa Fe Territorial Prison. By this point, blood poisoning had already begun to move through his body, and he died four days later. He was buried in Santa Fe.

Sam never made a statement about the crimes and exited this world without seeing his brother again. The news traveled around New Mexico and Texas, but Black Jack was somehow ignorant of the robbery or his brother's death in prison. In those days, if one didn't happen to be in a town or have access to a newspaper, he missed current news entirely. One thing is certain: if he had been informed, he never would have robbed the same train. Yet just a month later, he went for it alone and was shot in the right arm by the conductor. The blow was an incredible force, essentially tearing his arm off. In excruciating pain, he went into shock. The conductor left him to bleed out on the side of the railroad tracks and carried on to the next stop to notify officials. Blood drained from his lifeless body, and the chance of survival was slim. It wasn't his time though—his fate would be even worse. He was found, given medical treatment, and eventually transported to the Clayton County Jail. His sentencing to death by hanging came promptly.

The news surrounding his impending execution spread throughout the nation. The man who had terrified countless train passengers and robbed without mercy was now set to die. Posters were printed, tickets were sold, and the townspeople were eager for the spectacle. It may seem peculiar that they were rather excited, but Clayton had never been the center of this sort of attention. Black Jack became more of a celebrity than a criminal.

On the morning of April 26, 1901, crowds formed outside of the courthouse as Black Jack awaited his execution. His outward persona seemingly surprised onlookers, for his behavior was later characterized as strikingly nonchalant. Although he was shackled, he projected an unusual courage in the face of death. He requested some music, and they sent for a violinist who played while he ate his final meal. When he was asked at what time he wished to die, he responded, "Oh, any time before noon. I'd like to be in hell for dinner." His demeanor appeared jovial with reporters, and he provided them with amusing responses to their questions. As the hour grew nearer, a priest came to his side, and he spent time talking with him. He

Black Jack Ketchum on the gallows, prior to his hanging in Clayton, New Mexico. *Harry M. Rhoads, 1901, Denver Public Library Special Collections.*

admitted that he had allowed other men, who were currently locked up in Santa Fe, to endure the fall for some of his own crimes. This seemed to press on his conscience because in the days prior, he wrote a letter to the president about his desire for their release. He also claimed that while he had robbed countless people, he never killed a man.

It was precisely 1:17 p.m. when he was led to the scaffold. He stood beside the priest, witnessed by hundreds of excited faces. Death may have been more preferable to the anxiety he surely experienced throughout the morning. With no escape from his doom, the rope was placed around his neck. "Good-bye," he said, and "please dig my grave very deep." A black sack was brought over his face, making the crowd and the glare of the bright sunlight disappear underneath it. He shouted, "Let her go!" The show was almost over, and within seconds, he would be dead. However, his death wouldn't come as quickly as everyone assumed.

According to a report made the following day in the *Herald Democrat*, "The body shot through the trap, and the head was torn from the trunk by the tremendous jerk. The head remained in the sack and fell into the pit. The body dropped to the ground quivering and bleeding. Some men groaned and others turned away, unable to endure the sight. The blood issuing an intermittent stream from the several arteries, as the heart kept on with its mechanical beating." Witnesses toward the front of the crowd had splotches of Black Jack's blood on their own bodies. From that point forward, Clayton would be associated with this horrific botched hanging.

Terror pulsated through the gathering of spectators. According to witness accounts, some screamed, while others were stunned into silence. They had watched a living, breathing man beheaded as if he was in a barbaric guillotine. The body lay lifeless, hunched over for several minutes, before it was removed from view. Considered only decent, his head was sewn back onto his body before the burial.

In the coming days, when the reporters all left town, Clayton became quiet again. The headlines faded from the newspapers before the dirt above his grave had even settled. All that remained was the record of a terrifying event. Any town with such a stain would want to blanket the memory. Except some hushed tales live on and linger out there in the emptiness, where his restless ghost may still ride alongside the lonesome tracks. The only man ever sentenced to death by hanging for train robbery in New Mexico was Black Jack Ketchum—the first and the last.

The Mysterious Blue Hole of Santa Rosa

In the midst of a rather flat basin that defines Santa Rosa's panoramic view, a natural pool of supreme clarity reflects the skies above. As a looking glass peering into the past, its depths contain histories leading back to the ice age. The surface has mirrored centuries of faces who stared into its abyss. Reaching back into the ripples of time, the Blue Hole quenched the thirst of Indigenous people roaming the terrain thousands of years ago. They saw it as a place with no other explanation than that of the divine. In later years, the eye of blue observed the coming of pioneers and cowboys, who bathed in its cool waters on their way across a daunting desert. A welcome sight and refuge it was for those making difficult journeys through this unforgiving land.

Beginning around the mid-1930s, when Route 66 came through Santa Rosa, it became a popular tourist destination off the highway. On any given summer afternoon, the Blue Hole is a refreshing oasis for people to take a

The Blue Hole, Santa Rosa. *Jessica Laughlin.*

dip under the warm sun. Kids splash and dare their friends to jump off the surrounding ridges. Picnics are held under the shade of cottonwood trees. To someone unaware of its age-old significance, it could be seen as just a pond—while pretty, it was nothing out of the ordinary. However, underneath this circular hole of brilliant cerulean water lies a fascinating mystery that delves into the depths of the earth.

When entering the area, bold white letters handwritten onto a wooden sign read, "Blue Hole, Depth 81 ft. Diameter 60 ft. Outflow 3,000 gallons per minute, Water Temp 61°." This description appears simple enough until one really begins to think it over. How does this particular body of water maintain a constant temperature of sixty-one degrees? Furthermore, how does it generate three thousand gallons of water every minute, as if set on some natural timer? The water is always fresh in the Blue Hole because every six hours, it becomes an entirely new pool of water. The hole is always in a state of rejuvenation. *Where* does the water come from?

The inner structure is similar to an hourglass—wider at the top, slightly narrowing in the center, and broadening again toward the bottom. Divers often find various objects left behind on the rocks, and a few fish have adapted to swim among them as well. At the edge of the floor, a slight opening in the limestone presents as a dark void, just large enough for a single person to swim through. This ominous entryway begins a narrow, ever-evolving cave system, leading to the unknown. Part of the cave's many passageways were explored to a depth of approximately two hundred feet. This marks the farthest anyone has ever descended. Expert scuba divers attempted to breach the labyrinth farther, but several have died during their investigations.

Part of the reason the cave stays impenetrable is that, upon entering, any movement against the limestone releases debris, almost completely reducing visibility to zero. Through the murky darkness, the only way out is to use ropes that serve to guide divers back to the surface. There is also the danger of getting caught in tight confines of the limestone. This, of course, would cause anyone to panic, even the most capable of divers. In moments of stress, the lungs need more oxygen, which increasingly drains the limited supply in their tanks. Because of the fatalities within the cave, a metal grate has since been installed as a barrier. The risk to life outweighed the curiosity, thus keeping the Blue Hole a mysterious and bottomless wonder.

Humans have made incredible advancements in our understanding of the universe beyond, but this same progress has not been seen in regard to the subterranean layers of our planet. Throughout New Mexico, entryways into the underworld exist in abundance, including one of the largest caves in the world, Carlsbad Caverns. Some theories suggest that the Carlsbad Caverns, roughly two hundred miles to the south, somehow connect to the caves of the Blue Hole. We may never know the answer. Removed from the light of day, these places are both menacing and extraordinary. They have their exploratory limits due to the volatility. Still, humans continue to push these boundaries in a quest for better knowledge about the inner workings of our world.

What is known about Santa Rosa's topography is that it rests within a geologic marvel, termed the Santa Rosa Sink. The landscape around the city slopes downward at the rim, creating a basin, encircled by sandstone and overlaying soft limestone. The entire city is within a portion of the six-mile-diameter sink. Various spots, like the Blue Hole, have dissolved further due to rainwater softening the porous rock over time and leading to sinkholes of different sizes. The lakes and streams produced by this natural occurrence reveal subterranean water from a seemingly indefinite source. For instance, the water at the surface of the Blue Hole today may have been rainwater from thousands of years ago. This is also why Santa Rosa is considered the "City of Natural Lakes." Enjoyed by thousands each year, the Blue Hole greets visitors in the same humble way it has since its ancient beginnings. In the Land of Enchantment, perhaps some secrets are meant for the imagination.

The Jornada del Muerto on the El Camino Real

Deserts can be merciless. Long stretches of isolated desert, dry as bone, can make even those traveling by car nervous. They seem to evoke feelings of impending doom on a primeval level, as they lack basic essentials for survival. They are also beautiful in their own right. Their loneliness is somewhat poetic. Part of the Chihuahuan Desert, the Jornada del Muerto is a section of extreme desolation. This was especially true in the early seventeenth century, when Spanish explorers set the path of the El Camino Real.

The El Camino Real, the Royal Road, was a trail from Mexico City to Santa Fe. Much of this corridor followed alongside the Rio Grande, providing access to water. A feared segment of this route, however, veered away from the protection of the river and treaded north through the Chihuahuan Desert. To cross this empty land of ninety miles usually took upward of a week or two. Caravans frequently traveled by night to avoid the sun in the spring and summer months, when temperatures reached above one hundred degrees. In the winter, it was equally as miserable to traverse in the frigid cold, rain, and snow. Therefore, preparing to cross was critical, and failure to plan for broken wheels, sickness, or other setbacks was lethal. They also had

Riding into the Jornada del Muerto. *Jessica Laughlin.*

to load their carretas with canteens of water to last throughout the arduous trek, for themselves as well as their horses and oxen.

In addition to all of these factors, there were ruthless patches of quicksand. A man could be pulled downward to his knees in seconds and, without receiving prompt help, buried alive. In this scenario, the desert gripped at the living, dragging its victims into the ground without warning. When a wagon began to sink in quicksand, the effort to lift it out was grueling. If one happened to be extremely unlucky during this battle, a torrential rain might make the process even more grim. Countless men, women, and animals died or vanished crossing the Jornada del Muerto. In the fight against the forlorn desert, the desert often won, imprisoning souls forever in a place where few birds fly.

One of the worst of the desert's casualties was in late September 1680, when 574 Spanish colonists of the Santa Fe region succumbed to their deaths attempting a voyage back to Mexico. Preceding their demise was an important uprising, the Pueblo Revolt. The Pueblo peoples in and around Santa Fe had been exploited by the conquistadors and settlers since 1607, when Santa Fe was colonized under Spanish rule. Pueblo Indians were harshly treated, and resistance was met with brutal imprisonments, whippings, or murders. A brave leader, Po'Pay of the San Juan Pueblo, seeking revenge and having been the victim of this brutality himself, coordinated an uprising. Nearly all of the Pueblo communities in the region participated. The mayhem that occurred in Santa Fe, including the burning of churches, successfully pushed Spanish settlers out.

Seeking refuge against the attack, already injured and sick, the colonists were forced to travel over the desert to safety in El Paso, Mexico. During the prolonged excursion of nine days, their illnesses and wounds made them susceptible to the elements. By the time the caravan of almost 2,000 souls finally arrived in El Paso, roughly 574 had died. Mexico's governor, Antonio de Otermin, described their final journey as the "Journey of Death." The name stuck, as did the desert's reputation. Over time, it became known as the "Dead Man's Journey." This significant defeat humbled Spain for twelve years. Yet the unbroken determination of the Spanish Crown would again lead to its rule of Nuevo México beginning in 1692, when Diego de Vargas reclaimed Santa Fe with military strength.

For years to come, the Jornada del Muerto remained the primary way into the northern territory. On its southern end, the neighboring towns of Mesilla and Las Cruces, along the Rio Grande, sprang into existence toward the end of the 1840s. Because they were far to the south, in the time following the Mexican-American War, both countries felt that the towns were within their boundaries. New territorial borders were confusing on the maps, and therefore this small strip was often called "No Man's Land." The Gadsden Purchase in 1854 finally resolved the issue, when the United States paid Mexico for an additional slice of land in present-day southern Arizona and New Mexico, which included these towns.

During this period, the El Camino Real became an important trade route, and so the Jornada del Muerto was again part of the story—

On the Old Trail through Mesilla, New Mexico. *Jessica Laughlin.*

The flamenco dancer. *Jessica Laughlin.*

frequented by vaqueros traveling north to Santa Fe and traders heading south to Chihuahua, Mexico, to sell goods. Mesilla and Las Cruces were at a confluence of intermingling cultures, long-awaited havens for travelers, where lovely señoritas danced, spinning their skirts into a whirlwind under sparkling stars. Tequila was poured freely at overflowing cantinas. Most carried a gun, and they weren't so afraid to use it. When a drunken man lost a hand at poker, he was liable to aim a pistol at his rival. Shots were fired in reckless abandon on the streets of old. So far removed from it all, this frontier close to the border had few laws.

While the Jornada del Muerto is for the most part dry, mesquite shrubs and yucca are scattered throughout the wilderness. What so many had failed to realize was that the sandy groundcover held water underneath its layers of lava rock. In 1867, the first well was dug in the center of the desert by ranching pioneer John Martin. The process took him two years, but he eventually hit water as he neared one hundred feet down. The well proved that development was possible in this hostile, parched land. He then brought in cattle, and the Aleman Ranch became a respite for many travelers on the El Camino Real.

While some people followed in his path, homesteading parts of the desert basin presented challenges. Larger communities never developed because of the difficulties. In the late 1800s, hot springs were discovered by settlers to the west of the desert, near the Rio Grande. This was a portion of land too challenging to travel by caravan when the El Camino Real was originally forged, and so it was bypassed, with the route directly cutting through the desert. The pools of mineral waters became an appealing attraction, and the town of Hot Springs was established. In the 1950s, the name was changed to Truth or Consequences, and it continues enticing visitors to soak in the calming waters of its spas.

In marched the twentieth century. Because of the area's isolation, the world's first atomic bomb was detonated as a test performed by the government in the Jornada del Muerto at the Alamogordo Bombing Range on July 16, 1945. The change in warfare stemming from this nuclear experiment would be like nothing the world had ever seen before. More recently, the land has become a base for commercial space exploration, with rockets launching into the vibrant blue skies above the San Andres Mountains. While these moments of discovery have been met with bewilderment by mankind, the desert remains indifferent to our advances. From the conquistadors to the Space Age, exploration continues here in the most adverse of environments. After all, the past five hundred years are but a speck of sand in time to a desert of ancient origins.

The Discovery of Carlsbad Caverns

The Guadalupe Mountains extend across West Texas into southeastern New Mexico. Their dramatic jagged peaks and canyons were formed around 265 million years ago. During this bracket of time, called the Permian Period, a giant reef of living organisms was immersed in a vast sea. Being surrounded by land and connected to the ocean by only a slender channel made the sea vulnerable to Earth's changes. When the channel was ultimately cut off from the ocean, evaporation occurred over time. The reef was eventually exposed to the light of day. Infinite mounds of shells and skeletons from organisms once thriving underwater here created the limestone rock through complex processes and release of lime. Evidence of life may be found in the primitive fossils of shellfish and sponges embedded into the sediment. Ancient lifeforms, some extinct, created the very home now inhabited by snakes, lizards, squirrels, and bats. Ammonite shells, tucked securely into the limestone walls, remind us how young we are in comparison. Their swirling patterns, intricate and symmetrical, seem to symbolize the always revolving Mother Earth.

Geologists often consider Capitan Reef to be the greatest prehistoric fossil reef in the world. Because the area was once covered in water, the surface below is rich in oil and gas. This is why the flat Permian basin of West Texas is covered in oil rigs. It is this same oil that made Carlsbad Caverns' formation unique compared to other caves. Most caves form as a result of rainwater entering through cracks in rock and eroding over time. The process was slightly different within the Guadalupe Mountains, where oil and gas residues created hydrogen sulfide. Combined with regular water, the concoction resulted in sulfuric acid. Fragile limestone easily erodes in acidic environments. Abundant rainwater seeped through the reef to design the labyrinth of chambers within the layers of fossilized rock.

Petroglyphs in the Guadalupes, carved into mountain walls by early man, reveal hunting scenes and other imagery. A type of red paint was used to create pictographs. It's incredible that these works of art exist to tell basic stories stretching as far back as four thousand years ago. These Native people knew about the caves because their art is found near the entrance and throughout the backcountry. However, within the cavern, signs of primitive man are scarce. So the history of actual exploration within the cave begins much later, at the turn of the twentieth century.

In 1898, a sixteen-year-old cowboy, James "Jim" White, was working as a ranch hand near the Guadalupe Mountains close to the Texas–New Mexico border. On this particular spring evening, he noticed what appeared to be a plume of smoke billowing from the horizon. He hopped onto his horse, riding quickly to gain a better view. As he approached the scene, he gazed above to a swarm of bats flying against the twilight. Mesmerized by their flight, he watched them for hours until they receded into the mountainside. In his own words, Jim recalled the moment he saw the cave entry for the first time: "I worked my way through the rocks and brush until I found myself gazing into the biggest and blackest hole I had ever seen, out of which the

Jim White discovers the Carlsbad Caverns. *Jessica Laughlin.*

bats seemed literally to boil. I couldn't estimate the number, but I knew that it must run into millions." To gauge the depth of the cave, he lit a fire on a branch and went to the cave opening. Throwing it into the hole, it seemed to drop into eternity, giving him a sense of how massive the cave was. He kept the secret to himself initially, returning to examine its entrance further in the coming days.

Only the bravado of a teenager, possessing a curiosity to match, could have embarked into this vast emptiness alone. With a lantern and ladder of wooden sticks, he cautiously entered the gap. He must have known this exploration to be unwise, but the bats and entryway didn't deter him. Peering into the hollowness, he determined that it was an enormous cave, and the light from his lantern illuminated hazy shapes of strange formations below. In the weeks ahead, Jim returned numerous times, becoming braver and more prepared with every visit. Realizing that it was outright foolish and dangerous to continue by himself, he told a friend, who joined in the expeditions. History never recorded his friend's name, but it is known that he was Mexican and spoke little English. The two steadily entered past the entrance using the rope ladder. If either one of them had taken a step too far over the ridge of each tier, he likely never would have been found.

When Jim set eyes on what he referred to as the "Big Room," he was overwhelmed by its magnificence. The grand chamber was decorated like a palace. It appeared as if he had discovered another world. The ceilings were adorned with natural chandeliers of speleothems that resembled icicles. Colossal mounds rose in all sizes from the floor, and some of these cone columns were so tall that they almost touched the drapery above. Drops of water occasionally echoed in the darkness.

The more he shared tales of the cave with others, the more his secretive realm became exposed. The first to see its potential was a fertilizer company that began mining bat guano. Jim was hired as a foreman, and this provided him ample time to develop paths into new chambers. Although the bat guano business was lucrative for his employer, Jim recognized the magic of the caverns and tried to protect it from too much damage. He also offered tours in his spare time to thrill seekers who weren't afraid to be lowered hundreds of feet in a bat guano bucket. Many chambers were named by Jim, including King's Palace and Papoose Room. When he eventually married, his wife, Fannie, would often participate in hosting visitors with a simple meal at the bottom of the cave. The couple shared a respect and love for this incredible underworld.

Exploring the Carlsbad Caverns. *Jessica Laughlin.*

It must have been frustrating for Jim trying to expand public awareness of the cavern's splendor. He had spent most of his life in the cave by the 1920s and knew that it had greater significance than as a bat guano producer. He concluded that the only hope the caverns had in gaining protection would

King's Chamber, Carlsbad Caverns, circa 1926. *Library of Congress.*

be found at the government level. After tremendous effort, President Calvin Coolidge designated Carlsbad Caverns as a national monument in 1923. Jim became a guide and sold his story for pocket change to visitors. Just a few years later in 1930, the caverns became a national park. Sadly, Jim never received the notoriety during his lifetime that he so rightfully deserved. He later explained the impact the caverns had on him: "The beauty, the weirdness, the grandeur and the omniscience absolved my mind of all thoughts of a world above. I forgot time, place and distance."

When he passed away in 1946, he at least knew that the caverns would endure for future generations. He was laid to rest beside Fannie, and his grave was inscribed, "The Discoverer of Carlsbad Caverns." In the nearby town of Carlsbad, a bronze statue pays homage to his explorations at the National Cave and Karst Research Institute. Since the founding of the national park, researchers have discovered well over one hundred caves and continue to delve farther into the extremities. One such exploration uncovered bones of a massive sloth in Devil's Den, a location directly below the natural entrance. These remains are considered to be 110,000 years old, and theories suggest that the sloth likely entered the cave by an accidental fall. Given the maze

James Larkin White. *Carlsbad Caverns National Park.*

of chambers, new discoveries are revealed, and the mysteries persist.

As each fall turns to spring, the Mexican free-tailed bats continue their transcendent migration pattern, returning to the caverns to give birth. They are the descendants of those Jim White witnessed in 1898. The only flying mammal, they darken the sky by the thousands each night, retreating to the cave's sanctuary to rest during the heat of the day. They tuck their wings into tiny bodies and hang from the ceiling of prehistoric limestone. Their babies are sheltered by the material of spiraling ammonites and other creatures that once found their refuge in the great Capitan Reef, when this land in New Mexico was under the sea.

The Life of Christopher "Kit" Carson

Christopher "Kit" Carson was a critical figure in American expansion in the West. He lived during the height of dramatically changing times and geographic boundaries. His image as a brave mountain man has been fixed into our history through decades of romanticized western narratives. This fascination with idolizing western legends began during his lifetime, when books and dime novels emerged in the 1800s. These novels turned men into the legends we still find intriguing today. The plight of cowboys on the open range, fighting against hostile Indians in the harsh elements, could be vicariously experienced through these short and exciting tales. To the reader living a predictable life, the West became synonymous with adventure. Kit Carson, the famous guide, became the hero in many of these tales. The problem with the fabricated plots, however, was that the hero of the story was typically a white man, and his desires were the only perspective valued. The Indian was portrayed as either submissive or an adversary. If they weren't providing some kind of assistance, they were usually considered a threat.

Some basic themes stemming from the stories were true. The West was dangerous territory. Thousands of settlers who embarked on the trails were killed due to a number of causes, from disease to attacks on their wagon parties. At the same time, Native people were facing an invasion of domineering powers unlike anything they had ever experienced. Comparable to a photograph taken in a fleeting moment, the full picture ultimately depends on what lens is used. Legends like Carson resemble a portrait slightly out of focus, leaving the details open to the viewer's interpretation of the facts. While he committed many heroic acts, he also did the contrary.

Carson was born in Kentucky on Christmas Eve 1809 into a large family. One year later, his parents relocated to central Missouri in a settlement called Boone's Lick, where the forests were thick along the Missouri River. Their main source of income was through farming, but his dad also built cabins. As early settlers to the region, they homesteaded on land recently occupied by Native tribes. This led to frequent raids on their property and their community. Farmers in this area built forts around their homes made of tall fencing to ward off attacks. As an impressionable boy, Carson learned to defend himself during moments of strife. He also recognized the complexities of various tribes and his own family's relationship among them as they tried to coexist.

When he was eight years old, his father, Lindsey, abruptly died from a fallen tree while working to clear a field. His mother, Rebecca, was left to fend for herself, and Kit grew up fast in the wake of this misfortune. After the death of his father, their poverty worsened. He became occupied with caring for the land and helping raise his younger siblings. Because of his newfound responsibilities, he never learned to read or write. When his mother remarried, Carson was an adolescent and developed a bad relationship with his stepfather. The conflict between them was too draining on the household, so Rebecca thought of an alternative for her son. She decided to send him to Franklin, Missouri, where he would be an apprentice to a saddlemaker. For obvious reasons, this might have caused him to feel rejected, but it also enhanced his independence.

Franklin had become an important hub for those setting off on the Santa Fe Trail. Since the trail officially opened a few years prior, Franklin's downtown was booming with business. Kit watched from the window of the shop as fur trappers, traders, and settlers rode through town. His hands grew tired of stitching, and he yearned to be among them instead. The temptation burned inside of him to see what awaited beyond. Franklin was considered more of a starting point, so most people passing through were full of confidence and hopeful about their journey ahead. Mountain men, dressed in fur jackets and beaver hats, told stories of their experiences upon

Kit Carson in the wilderness. *Jessica Laughlin.*

their return. Shy but always listening, Kit absorbed it all. After about two years as an apprentice, he decided that it was high time to leave. He knew that his fate didn't end in Franklin, but rather somewhere out in the distance. Without providing a reason to his mentor, he took off on the fabled trail into the Southwest with a caravan of trappers.

He was considered a runaway, but nobody seemed to care. To prove himself useful, he tended to their horses and helped with odd jobs. Once in Santa Fe, he decided to venture north to Taos. Inhabited primarily by Mexicans and Natives, it was also a gathering place in the winter for fur traders. Soon thereafter, he was taken in by Matthew Kinkead, an old friend of his father's from Kentucky. Kinkead was a mountain man and helped shape Carson's understanding of the profession by teaching him how to hunt and survive in the wilderness. Along with these skills, he acquired different languages to interact better with the Spanish and French. He then began accompanying hunting brigades farther into remote territories. Once he demonstrated his loyalty to the other men, he became a valuable member of their society.

Life as a mountain man was treacherous and deadly. They endured the extremes of faraway lands few Americans had ventured into before and utilized their wits just as often as their rifles. Under the guidance of these men, who were oftentimes as untamed as the wildlife they pursued, Carson grew into a man. These early trappers were some of the first white men to interact with Indians. Bands of Natives would sometimes ambush them at their camps. They could also make peace just as rapidly by trading goods, and long-standing relationships were formed. Native people shared their knowledge with mountain men about tanning buckskins, drying meat, and the benefits of camping in tipis. Just as diverse tribes fought among themselves, they all had their own friends and enemies. These men oftentimes became so close with various tribes that they wed Native women and completely immersed themselves in their culture.

Each year, a rendezvous occurred in the remote Northwest, and it was commonly held on the Green River in present-day Sublette County, Wyoming. Rendezvous were similar to flea markets, where Native tribes and fur traders bartered commodities. At dusk, the gathering would turn into a party, where everyone drank and danced beneath the Milky Way. During one of these nights, by the glow of a bonfire, Carson laid eyes on a beautiful Arapaho woman by the name of Waa-nibe, "Singing Grass." Their attraction was dynamic, and she immediately captured his heart. He fell in love for the first time, and they married. They roamed the valleys together, and she birthed their first child, Adaline, in 1837. In southern Colorado, they lived among her tribe. Singing Grass was taken from him merely two years later, days after the birth of their second daughter.

Widowed with a new baby and toddler in his care, he headed to Bent's Fort on the Santa Fe Trail in what would become southeastern Colorado. The fortress was made of adobe and served as a trading post. Hundreds of people worked at the fort, and Carson became employed as a hunter. Every traveler along the trail stopped there to stock up on supplies needed for the barren section ahead. The Cheyenne and Arapaho sold plenty of goods as well and lived near the fort. This was beneficial to Carson, as he was supported by the Native women in raising his girls. He soon met Making-Out-Road, from the Cheyenne tribe. They eventually married, but their union dissolved within the year. His youngest daughter passed away during this time. Carson knew that the wild life of a frontier outpost was no place for Adaline, who was now growing older and needed a stable home life. With limited options, he arranged for her to be cared for by his sister near St. Louis, Missouri, in 1842.

On the return trip, after parting with his daughter, Carson went west by steamboat on the Missouri. Now in his thirties, he was unsure of the path forward. It was then that his next chapter was revealed when he met another passenger on board, John C. Frémont, an officer of the U.S. Topographical Corps en route to his first major surveying expedition. Frémont realized how valuable Carson could be to his small team. Aware of the dangers in the frontier, he offered him a job to be his scout. Without much hesitation, Carson accepted the offer.

Their first expedition explored the Wind River and South Pass of Wyoming. This region cut through the Continental Divide in the Rocky Mountains but was smoother terrain. It would become a path traveled by settlers on the Oregon Trail, for it was easier to navigate. They encountered and overcame several difficulties together during this first voyage. In Frémont's journals, he often praised Carson, expanding him into a legendary figure. In his later book, *Memoirs of My Life*, he gave his first impression of Carson: "He was a man of medium height, broad-shouldered and deep-chested, with a clear steady blue eye and frank speech and address; quiet and unassuming." Without Carson by his side, he certainly could have met an early death. Frémont leaned on Carson's survival instincts in tense situations. After the assignment, Frémont's journals were converted into a book, which gained overwhelming public attention. Having been two obscure men before the trip, they suddenly

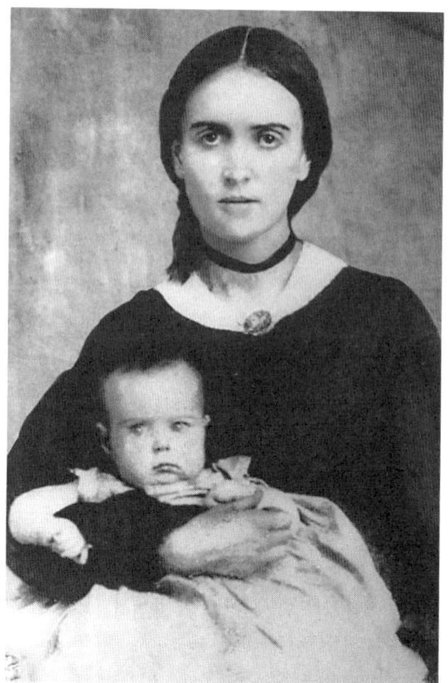

Left: John C. Frémont. *Author's collection.*

Right: Maria Josefa Jaramillo Carson with one of their children. *Author's collection.*

were national sensations. The fame was conflicting, though, because the pressure to meet the expectations of the public was burdensome.

Before the expedition, he was introduced to Maria Josefa Jaramillo of Taos by her brother-in-law, Charles Bent, who owned Bent's Fort. Her loveliness lingered on his mind during the six months he spent away. Upon returning, he went to Taos, where he intended to reside and win the affection of Josefa. After he converted to Catholicism to gain her parents' approval, they were married in Our Lady of Guadalupe Church in Taos on February 6, 1843. She was fifteen and he was thirty-three, but the age difference wasn't uncommon during the nineteenth century. They purchased a modest adobe house near the Taos Plaza, but just as he was settling into domestic life with his new bride, he was once again asked to join Frémont on another mission.

For several years and on three missions, Carson crisscrossed the West with Frémont and his party of roughly thirty men. The group scaled mountainsides, plodded through raging rivers, endured the thirst of empty deserts, outlived near starvation, suffered the biting snow of the Sierras, and fought off frequent strikes against them. They also just so happened to be in California during the eruption of the Mexican-American War, where they evolved from explorers into trailblazers of the U.S. occupation. In 1846, they were present at the uprising of American settlers in Sonoma, California, known as the Bear Flag Revolt. Time and time again, Carson proved himself to be the most fearless of men. At practically every turning point of western expansion during the 1840s, Kit Carson was there. Because of his endeavors, the maps produced by Frémont's topographers served as the gateway west for thousands of migrants thereafter.

While Carson was in California, the Taos Revolt occurred. Charles Bent, the newly elected governor of the New Mexico Territory, was attacked by a militia of Mexican and Native men. Bent was married to Josefa's sister, Ignacia, and the two families were extremely close. Josefa often stayed with them and happened to be present when the murder occurred on the morning of January 19, 1847. The women and children escaped and were unharmed. Carson was unaware of Bent's death until he returned to Taos several months later to find his family torn apart by grief. When he heard the story, he was infuriated and extremely saddened by the loss. The couple later named their firstborn son Charles Bent Carson in his honor.

His extensive absence in the prior years had little effect on the couple's fondness for each other. Having spent much of their marriage on the frontier, Carson wanted to stay close to home. This led him to seek employment

Kit Carson's house in Taos, New Mexico. *Jessica Laughlin, 2025.*

with the government as an Indian agent in Taos. He intended to serve as a peacemaker between the United States and tribal nations, but ultimately, the decision would test his own morality.

As a man who cherished the freedom of the West, he soon became indistinguishable from those who were attempting to tame it. After briefly serving in the Civil War for the Union and uniting the first New Mexico Volunteer Infantry, he was promoted to lieutenant colonel. He fought in two significant battles against the Confederates at Battle of Valverde and Glorieta Pass. Now distinguished in war, his services were then sought for another purpose under the direction of General James Carleton.

Carson was ordered by Carleton to detain all of the Navajo in 1863. He wanted to force their relocation from their home around the four corners region to the distant Bosque Redondo reservation in eastern New Mexico. Carson knew that the task would be too problematic. While he agreed with a form of reservations, he thought they should be located within the homelands of the tribe's territory. Knowing that the government's plan would lead to disaster, he firmly resisted the commands by submitting his resignation. For several months, he remained in Taos, but Carleton continued to pressure him. Maybe he was loyal to a fault or he had no way out, but he eventually gave in to the general.

The Navajo homeland was an expansive swath of unique terrain, including the breathtaking Canyon de Chelly and Monument Valley. As skilled farmers, they maintained fruitful valleys where rare peach trees lined lush fields. Residing beside the cliffs, they were a sturdy nation of thriving villages. They were also scattered, and their communities were spread throughout a large vicinity. Carson enlisted the help of Ute tribesmen who assisted his soldiers in the effort. The Navajo were given warnings beforehand and abandoned their homes for the respite of the canyons. They assumed that if they could wait long enough, the army would leave. This worked at first. However, Carleton's orders became increasingly demanding in the following months, and he established a scorched-earth policy. In an effort to bring the Navajo out from hiding, Carson's army was required to destroy crops, burn villages, kill livestock, and leave nothing behind other than charred ground. These actions didn't fit his character, and he attempted once again to request a leave of absence. This was refused. During the winter, the Navajo were given no other choice than to reveal themselves due to starvation and illness. They knew that it was only a matter of time in the cold before death would take them all.

The Long Walk of the Navajo. *Jessica Laughlin.*

Around eight thousand Navajo surrendered to the army and were forced to walk four hundred miles across New Mexico. Women carried infants on their backs who cried of hunger, but their mothers had barely any strength to survive themselves. The elderly leaned on wooden canes as their bodies caved forward in agony. Men who had been warriors were stripped of dignity and forced to watch their families dehumanized in front of them. Although Carson returned to Taos and wasn't present for the entire shameful journey, he knew that he had caused their suffering. He had been strong enough to climb even the mightiest of mountains, but he was weak in the face of fighting for what he believed to be true. Not only was the Long Walk inhumane, but their eventual arrival at Bosque Redondo was also equally as appalling. The barren land was hostile and meant to be shared with their longtime rivals, the Mescalero Apache. There was not enough food, and the murky Pecos River was their only source of water. They were required to assimilate by giving up their own gods for Christianity. Soldiers often assaulted the women, further degrading their sense of self. Of those who lived through the brutal walk, many died after they reached the reservation. Some perished from malnutrition or sickness, others of broken spirits longing to return home.

Carson likely wanted to forget the experience, especially after he witnessed the reservation's conditions. His complicity in taking orders from Carleton would haunt him. Yet his service was met with praise by the military. The only one who didn't celebrate it was Kit Carson himself. He must have struggled internally to grasp what he had done to the Navajo. He even adopted a Navajo boy and raised him alongside the seven other children he had with Josefa. Never able to truly settle, he continued on with his government service as a brigadier general at Fort Garland in Colorado, where his family was able to join him in military housing.

Portrait of Kit Carson. *David F. Barry, Denver Public Library Special Collections.*

In 1868, Josefa experienced a traumatic birth with their last daughter. The loss of blood and complications caused her death within two weeks. Overcome by her passing and consumed with the task of raising their children, the stress began to take a toll on Carson's already deteriorating health. The following month, he died of an aortic aneurysm. The man who rode on the narrowest rims of the West and survived against it all could not battle the pain of his own broken heart. The place he loved most, with its uncultivated lands, was forever gone, and he had led the way.

El Santuario de Chimayo

In the small village of Chimayo, located beside the Sangre de Cristo Mountains, sits one of the world's most spiritual chapels. Surrounding this haven in the foothills are tranquil gardens shaded by canopies of mature trees. Behind the humble adobe church, the Santa Cruz River trickles over rocks and steadily flows through the foliage. In this holy place, natural beauty converges with the divine. There is the gentle rustling of leaves, water, and birds softly singing as they fly from branch to branch. El Santuario de Chimayo is alive with miracles and seemingly touched by the heavens.

Long before Chimayo became a renowned shrine, the riverfront property was owned by sheepherder, Don Bernardo Abeyta. He was a religious man and a member of the Hermanos Penitentes. The Penitentes were a secretive brotherhood, and membership to their organization was not granted to everyone. Devotion to Catholicism was at the root of their society, which was prevalent in the rural villages of northern New Mexico and southern Colorado in the early nineteenth century. The origins of the Penitentes may be traced to the remoteness of their villages and an absence of a traditional parish. While they were generally a charitable group who believed in building faithful communities, they also performed ritualistic ceremonies. These rituals involved acts of penance to atone for past sins and reenactments of the crucifixion of Christ.

The legend of Chimayo began on the night of Good Friday in 1810. The moon was full and shined on the river. On this evening during the Catholic Holy Week, Abeyta was worshiping with the Penitentes when he observed a glowing light coming from the ground near the edge of his property. He went toward it, and as he approached, the light appeared to be centered on one spot. Having strong faith, he knew that this was a sign from God. Kneeling on the ground, he began to inspect the soil that was now illuminated. Digging deeper, he felt something firm and wooden. A cross was revealed.

Although the heavy cross took some effort to lift, he placed it into the ground where the light was beaming. His Penitente brothers were as stunned

as he was to see the cross now upright and fully aglow. With the principal Catholic parish in the region located eight miles west of Chimayo in Santa Cruz, they determined that it should be transferred there at once. The priest was notified of the miraculous discovery the next day. He was also convinced that it must be a message from God. The cross was brought to the Church of Santa Cruz de la Cañada and placed above the altar. To his astonishment, the following morning, Abeyta found that the cross was again seated in its original hole. Bewildered, he still assumed that it should rightfully be displayed in the church. The cross was returned again, but the same baffling event transpired. Having done this three times to no avail, it was clear to all where the cross truly belonged. The story spread throughout the village, and worshipers came to visit what they called "el Pocito." Healing of ailments and answered prayers began to occur for those who visited the shrine.

Opposite: El Santuario de Chimayo. *Jessica Laughlin.*

Above: Don Bernardo Abeyta at the cross in Chimayo. *Jessica Laughlin.*

View of El Santuario de Chimayo. *Jessica Laughlin, 2022.*

The Native residents of the area heard about the discovery of the cross; however, they were not as surprised as the Catholics. They knew all along that the hills had healing powers. It was their belief that long ago there were hot springs, which dried out over the years. As with other hot springs in New Mexico, the water contained therapeutic qualities. Although the springs were no longer there, the remaining dirt was thought to be enriched with the antiquated minerals. For centuries, they rubbed the dirt of the hills on their bodies and ingested it for medicinal reasons.

While the Indigenous people held their own beliefs, they shared in the certainty that this site in Chimayo was blessed. Abeyta concluded that his sole purpose in life was to share the wonder of his discovery by building a church to house the cross. He spent the next few years seeking permission, and it was finally granted in 1813. The small chapel at the site of el Pocito was built first, and a few years later, the larger church was constructed next to it. The effort to build the parish was a labor of love by many artisans and inspired by their devotion.

Wooden doors open from the arched adobe walls of the courtyard, showcasing a picturesque view of the church, which may be best described as modest and lovely in the way it stands against a backdrop of rolling hills. Twin bell towers rise from each side, topped with crosses. The interior features folklore and religious sculptures known as "santeros." Decorated in ornamental "reredos," the altar features the original cross. Exposed wooden ceiling beams match the chiseled pews. Every detail was delicately handcrafted.

El Santuario de Chimayo welcomes thousands of people annually from all faiths. Some travel to Chimayo as a pilgrimage, and others come to be healed. The number of testimonies from those who claim that their prayers were answered after visiting the shrine is undeniably resounding. Numerous photos and crutches of the cured line the narrow walls of the original chapel. At the end of the room, a little doorway leads to another room containing el Pocito. The entry is so low that most visitors must bend to enter. The holy dirt may be taken as a remembrance. For more than two hundred years, this very hole in the ground has been the source of fulfilled miracles, and it's constantly replenished with holy dirt from the nearby mountains.

Throughout the week before Easter, and especially on Good Friday, thousands of people journey to Chimayo. For as far as one can see in the distance, they come by the droves, some carrying crosses over their shoulders while walking from as far away as Albuquerque. This tradition is mysterious but continues to endure. Transcending across cultures, generations, and faiths, this mecca along the High Road has become a symbol of the human spirit in the quest to unite with the heavens.

The Turquoise Trail

For centuries before the colonization of New Mexico, Indigenous people extracted the rare mineral turquoise throughout the Southwest. First mined by the Pueblo people more than one thousand years ago, ample turquoise was sourced from the Cerrillos Hills, located along what would later become the Turquoise Trail. The color was strikingly different against the otherwise southwestern palette of the region. With its blueish-green tone, they believed it represented the sky and water. This connection to the earth symbolized life, purity, strength, and protection to those who wore it. They also thought that turquoise was alive because of its ability to change color. Indeed, turquoise does alter due to its environment, affected by exposure to oils and water. Antique blue turquoise, exposed to oxidation over the years, becomes darker and takes on a greener hue. The mineral seems to age, as we do, changing over time and adopting new characteristics.

Once the Spanish arrived in New Mexico, colonists became interested in not only the turquoise but also the prospect of finding gold and silver in the Cerrillos Hills. Close to Santa Fe, the area was accessible to mining during the turn of the eighteenth century. Throughout the following decades, some silver was found, but nothing that would qualify as a true boom. Much later, placer gold was discovered in Tuerto Creek near the Ortiz Mountains in 1825. This brought a few camps to the area, and some villages began to emerge along the trail.

Once New Mexico became a U.S. territory, the area grew but remained an otherwise quiet region. It wouldn't be until 1879 that a major deposit of gold was unearthed by two prospectors from Colorado. Their lode generated an immediate boom, with hundreds of subsequent gold claims filed. The area saw the arrival of Spanish, European, and Italian settlers. The first railroad entered Cerrillos in 1880, which further boosted the influx of saloons, general stores, and hotels. The once tiny nearby settlements of Golden and Madrid flourished with new residents. Over the hills strewn with pinyon pines, and into the valleys below, they came in caravans hoping for a brighter future.

Boomtowns usually go bust at some point. The gold and silver boom was over within ten years as veins deep within the mountains began to run dry of the precious metals. However, the area managed to hold on to its population due to plentiful coal production near Madrid. Coal mining had its own set of tribulations. Mining families dealt with hardships that went hand in hand with working in the coal mines. They also faced pollution and less than desirable air quality from the coal production. Likewise, men were primarily the wage earners, so if they died in a mining accident, their families subsequently faced financial ruin. Madrid was a tight-knit community, though, and the owners of the mines valued their workers. They knew that the way to counterbalance the life of coal mining was to at least make Madrid a nice place to live. By the 1920s, the entire town was provided electricity from a company-owned power plant. At Christmas,

Caravans on the Turquoise Trail, New Mexico. *Jessica Laughlin.*

Madrid boasted the most dazzling of all light displays in New Mexico. Every household participated, and the streets were transformed into a winter wonderland.

Coal mining dominated the industry of the Turquoise Trail until the mid-twentieth century, when the coming of diesel engines caused the coal mines to become obsolete. Although the trail could have become a string of ghost towns, it made a comeback in the 1970s, when counterculture artists moved in for the inexpensive property. In the present, towns on the trail exude a mix of repurposed buildings, small cafés, galleries, and historical sites. It's an alternative path between Albuquerque and Santa Fe but well worth the extra miles off the interstate. Even though turquoise changes color with the worn effects of aging, it's still the same mineral. It renews itself again and again, just like this epic trail of old.

Billy the Kid

Most outlaws of the West were driven by desperation. Desperate men, women, and kids. None became more glorified than Billy the Kid, whose legend still rests somewhere between history and myth. A child hungry for more became a teenager desperate to belong. A charming gunslinger with a mischievous persona were necessities he possessed for his own survival. He had compassion for the underdog because he was an underdog himself. Those who took him under their wing were also hardened by life and circumstance. Having lost his father as a child, he gravitated toward outlaws, as those men gave him a place to feel safe. He was quick to protect those he cared about and to defend his stance against injustice. Billy's destiny wasn't necessarily by choice, but rather bred from the aching, ruthless world that he was forced to fight.

From the time he was a young boy, he was always on the run. Born Henry McCarty in 1859, he grew up in the overcrowded tenement buildings of an Irish immigrant neighborhood in New York City. Neighborhoods like Five Points in lower Manhattan during the 1860s were lousy with poverty and disease. Immigrants, such as his family, had moved from Ireland for opportunity in America, only to find their lives just as arduous in the city. There was not enough work, and if there was, they were paid poorly. This amplified crime and gangs. He learned as a boy to live by the law of none because the lawmen didn't seem to protect people like them; they had to fend for themselves. As he walked those streets, his childish blue eyes may have peered into a world of gray buildings, contrasted with lively and unpredictable streets. Kids with dirty shoes kicking old balls down the sidewalk may as well have been kicking poverty instead because laughter has the power to dull hunger. His parents may have had the desire to leave for a number of reasons, but it could have been simply wanting to start anew.

When Henry was around eight years old, his father died. Not much is known about the cause or place of his death. Some believe that he died in New York City, while others think it happened on their way to Indiana. Regardless of the timeline, the death of his father likely had an impact on his outlook. Without a solid income, his mother, Catherine, had her hands full in raising two boys; his brother, Joseph, was even younger than Henry. Once in Indianapolis, Catherine became a laundress, operating her own business. Working from sunrise to sunset, it's no wonder why she would grow tired from the load resting firmly on her shoulders. During these brief years in Indiana, she met William Antrim, who dabbled in a variety of professions but primarily was interested in mining. She liked him, but above all else, he could help her.

They decided to move to Wichita, Kansas, for land there was a good value. Catherine set up her laundry shop, and they bought some land with the expectation of becoming farmers. As soon as they settled into life on the plains, she began coughing up blood and could barely work without feeling completely run-down. The diagnosis was tuberculosis, which was practically a death sentence in those days. Doctors usually suggested that patients suffering from the disease move to an arid, high desert climate if they wanted to live longer. Much of the Southwest was populated by people who were trying to escape an early death from tuberculosis, and Catherine would be one of them—they headed into New Mexico on the Santa Fe Trail for this reason. Moving didn't seem to bother Henry, but running from place to place became his norm.

Once in Santa Fe, William and Catherine were married in 1873. They resided in the capital for a while but once again moved on to new horizons in Silver City, where a silver boom was happening. William's hope of striking it rich in mining was likely the reason for the move. After the family bought a cabin on Main Street, Henry attended school, which he thoroughly enjoyed. Not only did he find an escape by reading, but he was smart as well. It's been claimed that he could write with both hands, which would explain how he later could precisely use two guns in shootouts. He also learned Spanish because most of his friends were Mexican. Although William was his stepfather, he never bonded with him or looked up to him as a father figure. The two were regularly at odds, as William began spending nights away from home, which could have caused Henry to feel that his mother was being disrespected.

Catherine began to suffer not long after they arrived in Silver City. Tuberculosis was agonizing. Some could live for years with it lurking within, but once it fully erupted, it was usually dire. The coughing from the disease was exasperating, bringing up bloody phlegm, which poured from the mouth of the sick. Perhaps Catherine remembered the vast ocean she once saw before her as she crossed the Atlantic with nothing but hope of the American dream ahead. When she died, one can assume that the best part of Henry died too.

William didn't want anything to do with Henry after her passing. He had already moved on, and the boys weren't his obligation anyhow. Henry and Joseph were sent to foster homes, drifting further apart from each other. An orphan at fifteen, Henry was growing and hungry, which could have been the driving force behind him stealing a loaf of bread. Presumably, his clothes were also ragged and didn't fit right, leading him to take a basket of garments from a Chinese family's laundry business. For these petty crimes, he was caught and put in jail.

The sheriff could read between the lines though and had a soft spot for Henry. He was aware of his mother's untimely passing and that life was pretty tough on "the kid." This was notably his first time behind bars and confined to a jail cell. Perhaps something inside of him changed. Maybe he determined in those hours that while he didn't want to be a criminal, he wouldn't go hungry either. At the first opportunity, he managed to escape by climbing out of the jailhouse chimney. He stole a horse nearby and rode west, until he was far away in Arizona Territory.

Now in Arizona, he worked at various ranches, barely earning enough to feed himself. As he roamed around the territory, he met other outlaws and cowboys in saloons, where he played poker with his low wages. In 1877 at a Camp Grant bar, an encounter with a blacksmith, Frank Cahill, sent him over the edge. The two exchanged slights, and the feud grew antagonistic. When Cahill tried to tackle him to the floor, Henry pulled out his revolver and shot him in self-defense. He knew that he would be sentenced to die if he didn't leave Arizona immediately, so he rode back to familiar New Mexico as fast as he could.

Because he was still wanted in New Mexico, at some point he began going by the name of William H. Bonney. While there are several theories as to how

Billy the Kid. *Author's collection.*

he acquired this alias, there is no definitive answer. "Billy" was a common nickname for William, and therefore wanted posters referred to him as "Billy the Kid." Being labeled a killer was far worse than a thief, and his options were few. Somewhere out in the isolated expanse of southwestern New Mexico, he met Jesse Evans and his gang, "the Boys." Evans was in his mid-twenties and took a liking to the Kid. Rarely showing mercy to anyone else, he displayed some warmth, viewing Billy as a younger brother. He was impressed with his innate shooting abilities, which rivaled those of anyone in his gang. Around this time, Billy joined Jesse on their criminal escapades, like cattle rustling and robberies.

Despite his kinship with Jesse, the crew's actions were becoming more ruthless by the day. He continued to ride with them to their next stop in Lincoln County. Lincoln was already a town boiling hot from conflicts. The most pressing of these was the dispute between two businessmen who owned general stores on the same street downtown. To understand the turmoil, it's important to note here that New Mexico was influenced by a group of corrupt aristocrats known as the "Santa Fe Ring" in the mid-nineteenth century. This organization, formed by businessmen, politicians, and wealthy individuals, had their hands in projects throughout the new territory. They supplemented business ventures far from the capital, even in remote towns like Lincoln, where the Murphy-Dolan Store, also known as the "House," was in their pocket. They also controlled many of the lawmen, such as Sheriff William Brady.

The Ring didn't appreciate outside competition interfering with their monopolies. When English businessman John Tunstall, along with his partners Alexander McSween and John Chisum, set up shop in Lincoln, the action was perceived as a direct threat to their empire. Before this point, many of the farmers who supplied meat and produce to the Murphy-Dolan Store were paid in store credit versus cash, which forced the farmers to only shop at their store. Their total control of the area and its farmers spread broadly throughout Lincoln County, allowing Lawrence Murphy and James Dolan to become formidable men. Tunstall, on the other hand, was kinder to the farmers and offered to purchase their goods for cash. Misunderstanding the long-standing corruption in Lincoln, he proceeded to play fair in pricing and relationships in a place where fairness was nonexistent. Because of his better business practices, his store became favored among the townspeople. This infuriated Murphy and Dolan. The competition couldn't have come at a worse time for them, as the House was deeply in debt to the Ring.

Shortly after the outlaws arrived in Lincoln, they were hired by the House to settle the score with Tunstall. Both Billy and Jesse ended up getting thrown in jail on different occasions for robbing Tunstall's horses from his ranch. Since the sheriff was corrupt, they could break out just as easily as they were brought in. Tunstall knew that the only chance he had to save his business and his life was to form a posse of his own. Even though Billy had been a part of the horse thievery, he recruited him to join his fight instead. It wasn't a simple task for Tunstall nor an easy choice for the Kid to betray Jesse. Yet for Billy to find a way out of crime, he may have needed Tunstall just as much as Tunstall needed him. He was hired to help at his store and ranch but also as a bodyguard. While working for him, the two became close. Tunstall realized that Billy was skilled with a rifle and was also incredibly bright. Billy, now earning an honest pay, must have finally felt that his integrity aligned with his work.

The turf war soon reached dangerous heights. With old comrades, Jesse and Billy, on opposing sides, tensions were at an all-time high. Jesse's crew now went by the name the "Seven Rivers Gang." Even when they ramped up their violent tactics, they were never held accountable by the law because the sheriff was indebted to the House. All the while, Tunstall continued to pursue a truce among them and sought to persuade Jesse to join him as well, but his attempts failed. On February 18, 1878, while on his ranch, the twenty-four-year-old Tunstall was shot in the head by the outlaws. His entrepreneurial spirit in Lincoln had cost him his life. His death would lead to the Lincoln County War. Devastated by the murder, Billy and others who had worked for Tunstall came together to plot the destruction of the House. They were also supported by bands of Mexican farmers who had been victims of Murphy and Dolan's greed. They called themselves the "Regulators."

In the following months, the Regulators sought to avenge Tunstall's death by any means necessary. The events led to the bloodiest battle

Billy the Kid on the run. *Jessica Laughlin.*

between rival outlaws in the Southwest. To start it off, the Regulators fatally shot Sheriff Brady and one of his deputies outside Tunstall's store in April. After their murders, a slew of vengeful actions were taken against the House. The Seven Rivers Gang and the Regulators fought it out on the streets of Lincoln for five days in July 1878. The townspeople were terrified, locked up in their homes, with the constant sound of gunfire ricocheting from dawn until dusk. The newly hired sheriff, George Peppin, pleaded with the U.S. Cavalry to bring order to the anarchy. This was unheard of since the military rarely became involved in civil matters, but the unrest called for drastic measures.

The bloody battle resulted in the deaths of dozens of men on both sides. Held up in the McSween house, Billy and the others refused to leave, even when the soldiers demanded they evacuate. Ultimately, the Seven Rivers Gang set the house on fire with the Regulators inside. Flames engulfed the house, while they fought for hours until the bitter end. Having no choice other than to flee, the Regulators ran out the back door, shooting their guns. McSween along with numerous others were killed, but in the commotion, some escaped, including Billy. After all they had endured, it was Jesse who was most amazed by the Kid's getaway.

With McSween now deceased, the House had won. They reclaimed their domination of Lincoln. Their celebration didn't last long, though, because an aggressive cancer took the life of Murphy in October. All the fighting had benefited only Dolan, who would later purchase Tunstall's entire ranch for himself. Because of the disorder in Lincoln County and a change to New Mexico's government, a new sheriff, Pat Garrett, was appointed to bring a neutral rule of law to Lincoln. Once a buffalo hunter and one of the best gunfighters in the West, he was a man who had been on both sides of the law in the past. It's believed that he knew Billy and that the two were actually friends.

Portrait of Pat Garrett. *Author's collection.*

For roughly three years after the concluding battle in Lincoln, Billy's future was hanging in the balance. In hopes of putting an end to the fighting for good, Governor Lew Wallace provided pardons to the participants on both sides, but this excluded those who were subject to other criminal indictments. Billy wasn't granted amnesty because he was already indicted for the murder of Sheriff Brady. Still, he attempted to secure a deal with the governor through written letters; the governor promised forgiveness of his crimes if he would testify as a witness to another murder—one for which Dolan was the primary suspect.

The only reason Billy had information about this particular murder was due to a short-lived truce between the House and the Regulators, which occurred on the evening of February 18, 1879. This was exactly one year after the murder of John Tunstall. The meeting was prearranged in secrecy and intended to be an official end to the long-standing grudge. Following handshakes in the middle of the street, they all joined together for a disorderly night on the town. The peaceful gathering of heavy drinking took a turn when attorney Huston Chapman was shot by members of the House. The widow of Alexander McSween had hired Chapman to seek justice for her husband's murder during the Lincoln County War. Among others, Billy observed the callous crime firsthand.

Trusting the governor's word, Billy eventually surrendered. He appeared in court to testify, providing information that was used to bring charges against the men responsible for the murder, which included Dolan. For a variety of reasons, none of them was convicted. When days passed without a word from the governor, perhaps Billy's intuition was strong enough to realize that he had been given nothing other than false promises. Fleeing again from Lincoln, he found himself living in hiding and trailed by the law. The guaranteed pardon in exchange for his testimony was never granted. Billy was eventually captured once more and brought to trial in Santa Fe in April 1881. Even though so many other men had participated in the Lincoln County War, he was the only one convicted for any of the crimes.

Found guilty and sentenced to death, he awaited his hanging in Lincoln's jailhouse. It was there that he made his greatest escape. When only one guard was on duty, he managed to grab his gun and shoot him. He then took a long rifle, firing from a window to shoot another guard across the street, and unshackled his feet with an axe hanging nearby. Stealing a horse outside the jailhouse, he fled again. As a fugitive on the loose, Billy the Kid was now the most wanted man in the country.

Historical accounts claim that Garrett tracked Billy's whereabouts a few months later, in July, to Fort Sumner, New Mexico. Billy was there hiding out with his girlfriend, Paulita Maxwell, on her family's ranch. In the middle of the night, he was ambushed by Garrett and two deputies. Awakening to their raid, Billy was disoriented, shot twice, and killed. His body was promptly buried the following day, with few witnesses, in Fort Sumner's military cemetery. This was all believed to be true throughout Garrett's lifetime, and his fame rose alongside his career as a lawman. He wrote a book detailing the events that had transpired, but his storyline would come under question many years later in 1948.

It's hard to fathom that Billy the Kid could have lived in hiding well into the twentieth century, but a popular theory suggests that he survived until he was ninety. If this is true, it would mean that he lived through the coming of radio, television, airplanes and automobiles. He would have seen the Great Depression and World War II. It would also imply that Pat Garrett didn't kill the Kid but let him go instead, which introduces a variety of other questions with an infinite number of answers. The possibility that his life carried on for nearly seventy years after his alleged death is an enthralling allegation.

The sequel to the story begins when Jesse Evans disappeared around 1882. This was a year after Billy supposedly died. He was never seen or heard from again. Most assumed that he was probably dead, but others who knew him well may have been aware of his plan to vanish. Jesse Evans was missing until a strange story emerged in 1948 when an elderly man, Joe Hines, made some shocking statements to probate lawyer, William Morrison. They were meeting at the Hines home in Florida to sort out a land dispute. During their conversation about his inherited property, he revealed to Morrison that he was actually Jesse Evans and had been a part of the Lincoln County War. He also said that Billy the Kid was still alive and living in Texas under another pseudonym. This bit of information fascinated the lawyer, even though Hines wouldn't reveal Billy's alias or location.

Morrison went forward in researching his bold claims. His investigation brought him to another former member of the Seven Rivers Gang and a few other people who had known Billy. The revelations continued to surface, and everyone he spoke with similarly stated that Garrett didn't kill Billy. His research also brought about overlooked details, like how a photograph was never taken of Billy's corpse, which was a morbid albeit typical procedure when proving the execution of a wanted outlaw. The credible stories were compiled, eventually leading Morrison to Ollie "Brushy Bill" Roberts. The old cowboy had long resided with his wife in Hico, Texas. The community considered him to be a friendly sort who liked to tell stories about the frontier. Before being located by Morrison, he had never shared his identity as Billy the Kid with anyone, so he wasn't seeking fame in revealing his truth. He was apprehensive to speak to Morrison initially because he worried that if he confessed, he would find himself in trouble again with the law.

He agreed to expose his identity if Morrison would help him obtain a pardon from the New Mexico governor. In November 1950, a meeting was arranged with Governor Thomas Mabry. Roberts and Morrison assumed that it would be held in private, but when they arrived, it was a media frenzy. Some evidence pointed toward his story being plausible—his body showed more than twenty bullet and knife wound scars. In the end, though, the request for a pardon wasn't granted. The proof was not substantial enough to convince the governor, but proof was also tough to acquire since Roberts had lived as another man for decades. If he was in fact Billy, one can only imagine how disappointed he was to have never received a pardon. While walking down the street in Hico one month later, Roberts suffered a heart attack. He was buried in Hamilton, Texas, and his headstone reads, "Billy the Kid: William Henry Roberts."

Whether Billy died on that fateful summer night in 1881 in Fort Sumner, New Mexico, or in the midst of a twentieth-century winter in Hico, Texas, his legend endures. He remains in our collective thoughts as the youthful, wayward outlaw, on the dusty trails with guns blazing, riding forever into the setting sun.

PART II
ARIZONA

GERONIMO

Some people are born into lives ridden with loss. Geronimo was one of these unfortunate souls, and he lived somewhere in between the pain of his past memories and a constant desire to change the future for his people. Within No-doyohn Cañon in eastern Arizona, Geronimo entered his life in June 1829 along the rocky banks and soothing sounds of the Gila River. He became attached to the river, like those curling and exposed roots of the pines reaching toward the water. In his first days, he must have slept easily, as he was given the name Goyahkla, meaning "one who yawns." Perhaps he was saving his energy for later, when he would become the most courageous of all Apache leaders.

No-doyohn Cañon is the special place he considered to be his fatherland. While his people were often nomadic in nature, the Gila Mountains bordering New Mexico was where they returned home. As the fourth of eight children, he was raised within a large family. When they grew old enough to work, his brothers and sisters helped in the fields. They planted their crops in meadows that were tucked behind the cliffs. Some of what they harvested were rows of corn, beans, and melons. Herbs were also grown and used as medicine. Much like in any normal childhood, he ran through the fields with his siblings, climbed rocks, and swam in the river. They were taught Apache traditions and the importance of respecting the earth's rhythm and bounty. Beyond the shelter of their wigwams, their entire life was lived outdoors with the sun's reflection beating against the canyon walls.

Geronimo. *Jessica Laughlin.*

When Geronimo's father died after suffering from a long-term illness, it was his first true experience with death. He later explained in his autobiography, *Geronimo*, "His grave is hidden by piles of stone. Wrapped in splendor he lies in seclusion, and the winds in the pines sing a low requiem over the dead warrior." When an Apache husband dies, his widow typically remarries if she has children in her care. His mother never wanted to be with another man, so Geronimo took over the responsibility of providing for her.

Following in his father's footsteps, he became a warrior for the Bedonkohe band of the Chiricahua Apache when he was seventeen, under the command of Chief Mangas Coloradas. His admittance into the Council of the Warriors in 1846 was worn on Geronimo's soul with pride. His position as a warrior meant that he could also marry, and as he recalled, "Perhaps the greatest joy to me was that now I could marry the fair Alope, daughter of No-po-so. She was a slender, delicate girl, but we had been lovers for a long time." They settled into a wigwam near his mother's home, made of buffalo hides that were painted by his bride. As newlyweds, they shared dreams for their future and yearned for a family of their own. They were very much in love, and Alope was soon pregnant. The couple would have three sons in the following years.

At this point in time, their tribe was familiar with Mexicans but had rarely seen white men. The entirety of the Southwest was now under the territorial governance of Mexico, which had gained independence as its own country apart from the Spanish empire in 1821. The first Spanish missions in Arizona were established in the late 1600s near present-day Tucson, including San Cayetano de Tumacácori and the elaborate San Xavier del Bac. While other Indigenous communities throughout Arizona were subjected to forced oppression by the Spanish, the Apache homeland was initially farther out of their reach. They also aggressively fought against any intrusion into their strongholds with such ferocity that the incoming Spanish avoided such encounters. By inducing fear in their enemies through frequent raiding of settlements, the Apache were able to suppress Spanish dominance through violence.

Through the years and especially after Mexican independence, relationships between Mexicans and the Apache were ever evolving. For brief periods, there was temporary peace, but this never lasted long. The Apache had many communities, and so when one band had conflict with the Mexicans, generally all were blamed regardless of their specific tribal affiliation. Despite living relatively secluded lives when not on the warpath, they hadn't come to peace with the Spanish occupying their land in the first place. In their opinion, the land belonged only to them. The long-standing chaos and conflicting ideologies had been unfolding for years prior to the United States entering the region.

With a desire to expand the country from sea to shining sea during the mid-nineteenth century, the United States concluded that the land in between must be settled. This sparked migrations from the East and more bloodshed in the West. As the United States pressed forward, acquiring more territorial control over land that was owned by Mexico, the Mexican-American War in 1846 was the natural result. The Indigenous people throughout the area were facing threats from multiple fronts, and Geronimo found himself in the midst of a consequential time for his own tribe's survival. For some two years, the war was fought until it ended in 1848 in a U.S. victory. Mexico ceded much of its land, which then became most of the western United States. While the two countries came to an agreement, the boundaries with tribes were unclear. In 1853, with the Gadsden Purchase, the United States paid Mexico for another segment of land along the edge of the southern border, which made the situation even more tense for Natives.

During the summer of 1858, Geronimo's tribe went to trade across the Mexican border, as they felt the rapport with Mexicans had developed for the better. The distance required them to camp along the way. It was normal to bring women and children on such trips, but they remained in a guarded site while the men went into town to barter goods. Upon returning to their camp, the men arrived to find their campsite destroyed and many of their people killed. A few women who had managed to escape cried that Mexican troops had killed the guards before viciously attacking the women and children. Bodies lay scattered throughout the camp. Some were scalped and others beaten, shot, and stabbed. Remembering the horror, he explained, "I found that my aged mother, my young wife, and my three small children were among the slain. There were no lights in camp, so without being noticed I silently turned away and stood by the river. How long I stood there I do not know, but when I saw the warriors arranging for a council I took my place." In Apache tradition, it was forbidden to take the bodies of the dead, so they remained behind in Mexico on the field covered in blood and sorrow.

After walking back to their canyon for several days, Geronimo arrived at the empty wigwam he once enjoyed with Alope, where his children's toys were on the ground. He set it ablaze and then went to his mother's home to do the same. The human heart is fragile, but even when broken, it continues to beat on through the aching. In his later memoirs, he stated, "I did not pray, nor did I resolve to do anything in particular, for I had no purpose left." Those he loved the most were gone forever, and he vowed revenge against not only those responsible but all Mexicans indiscriminately. He barely ate, spoke, or slept for weeks. It seems as though he must have turned inward to find solace but found nothing other than his own misery. Onward he continued, but he wasn't the same again. The sight of the massacre lingered in his mind, as if it had burned into his vision like a permanent scar.

Along with Chief Mangas Coloradas, Geronimo sought support from other Apache in his plight for retaliation. Hundreds of Apache braves united to ride into the Mexican state of Sonora, eager to avenge the senseless murders of their innocents. Shortly after crossing into Mexico, they were met by soldiers as anticipated. The combat was brutal, as both sides fired shots, scalped, and stabbed their opponents with the sharpest of blades while attacking on horseback. After the Apache slaughtered all of the Mexicans, they encircled the dead soldiers and wailed cries for the avenged. Some theories suggest that Geronimo earned his name from the Mexicans' screams for the Catholic Saint Geronimo during times of battle, but this isn't confirmed.

Geronimo took pleasure in the revenge, but the retaliatory strike against the Mexicans didn't satisfy him. Relentlessly, he continued to pursue war south of the border. He returned too many times to count with his warriors, where they stole from the settlements. After ravaging through a community, they would return to Arizona to share what they gathered with their people. In Geronimo's mind, all Mexicans were to be tormented and pay for the crimes committed by some of their soldiers. They took the lives of both those in uniform and civilians alike. And just as the Mexican soldiers had taken women and children as hostages, they did the same. Geronimo later claimed that some of his people had been tied with chains for well over a year while being held as hostages in Mexico, but he noted that their own treatment of hostages was more humane.

All the while, new settlers were appearing in greater numbers. Originally, Chief Mangas Coloradas attempted to form a brotherhood with white men. He assumed since the United States had gone to war against Mexico, their shared enemy gave them common ground. However, he would find that just because he had positive encounters with them, not all shared the same intentions. Much like his son-in-law, Chief Cochise, of the Chokonen Chiricahua band of Apache, he was also betrayed. This led to increased hostilities that collectively became known as the Apache Wars, a series of battles between the Apache, United States, and Mexico.

Geronimo. *A.F. Randall, circa 1886, Library of Congress.*

To make matters worse, Mangas Coloradas was lured to Fort McLane in New Mexico to negotiate peace with military officers in January 1863. He was unusually tall for his time, over six feet in height. As he advanced toward the fort on horseback, he waved a white flag to signal his intent. This was disregarded; instead, he was captured and tortured throughout the night. His captives burned his feet and shot him multiple times. After he was dead, a physician severed his head for scientific purposes and sent it to New York City to be examined by Dr. Orson S. Fowler. He later wrote *Human Science of Phrenology* in 1873, which contained an illustration of his skull. The skull belonging to a prominent chief was put on display as an artifact, but eventually it went missing. This incident incited fury among all Apache.

The fire was burning hot on both ends. The Apache found it harder to escape their enemies, who were closing in on their whereabouts wherever they roamed. It appeared that the Native people in Arizona were a hindrance to the United States' ultimate goal of settling the West. Whether a tribe was amenable or aggressive was of little consequence to the government. Increased Anglo settlements were the priority, and it was thought that these wouldn't come to fruition so long as the Indians were free in the territory.

In our modern society, the insensible warfare committed throughout the Southwest during the nineteenth century is shockingly barbaric, but to appreciate the Southwest, one must understand the complexities of its past. All for the sake of land, thousands of people paid the ultimate price. The development of Indian reservations was considered to be a compromise, but in most instances, the confined were trapped in nothing more than a step above a prison.

The first of these was the Gila River Reservation, established in 1859. Both the Pima and Maricopa tribes shared this land. As skilled farmers, they grew and sold crops. The conditions on their reservation differed by many accounts from those at the San Carlos Reservation that followed in 1871. San Carlos was meant to become the designated homeland of the Apache, Mojave, and Yavapai. It became known as Hell's Forty Acres due to its severe reputation. The land was also less ideal to grow crops, and shortages of food led to famine. Officials operating the reservation also expected tribes to assimilate and denounce most of their own customs.

After the death of Mangas Coloradas, Geronimo assumed the position of chief. He avoided being taken to San Carlos until 1877 before he was captured by the U.S. Army. Once on the reservation, he remained there for four years before making an escape with others in 1881. He was successful in his first attempt and even better at hiding once he was free. While on the loose, he again raided settlements for most of his tribe's needed supplies. However, by then the population of white settlers in southern Arizona had increased dramatically. Frontier boomtowns like Tombstone and Bisbee were well underway. The way of life Geronimo had once understood was simply no longer the same. There were now lawmen on his trail, alongside the cavalry. Although he may not have been privy to his national fame while attempting to survive in the wild, his name was now branded throughout the country due to the presence of newspapers like the *Tombstone Epitaph*.

Coupled with the responsibility he felt for his people, the pressure to remain free must have been immense. He surrendered by returning to the reservation in 1884. Perhaps he was tired of running or maybe he needed to rest, but an eagle isn't content in a cage. Just one year later, he got away again with more than one hundred Apache. His second escape was an embarrassment to the United States and considered a risk to the nearby towns. General Nelson Miles sent five thousand troops to search for the renegade, but they had no luck in finding him for more than a year.

When Geronimo received the news that many from his tribe were sent from San Carlos across the continent to Florida, he felt defeated. The Apache who were hiding alongside him were sick with grief. They knew that if they didn't surrender, they would never see their relatives again. This was the defining moment when Geronimo and his remaining Apache surrendered at Skeleton Canyon on September 4, 1886. Upon their agreement, Geronimo said, "Once I moved about like the wind. Now I surrender to you and that is all."

As they stepped foot onto the Apache prisoner of war train bound for Florida from Holbrook, Arizona, Geronimo knew that he would never see his homeland again. Far beyond the flat horizon, towering cliffs near the Gila River still concealed the bones of his father. Although he likely thought that someday he would again be among the trees of his youth, it was all lost to Geronimo.

When they arrived in Florida, most were taken to Fort Marion, but Geronimo and other Apache were moved to Fort Pickens, where they performed manual labor for nearly two years. They were then transported to the Mount Vernon barracks in Alabama. With each move, fewer Apache survived. About 450 Apache were detained as prisoners of war. Many children were sent to the Carlisle Indian Industrial School in Pennsylvania to be further assimilated into white society. The mothers despaired and were unsure if they would hold their children again. Malnutrition and disease spread through the barracks. Many became sick due to a rampant surge of tuberculosis, including one of Geronimo's own sons, Chapo, who died from the illness in his twenties.

Because of the rapidly deteriorating conditions, they were relocated to Fort Sill, Oklahoma, in 1894. This would become their final home, and although they were imprisoned, they had more freedoms there than in Alabama. Gradually, they cultivated the land. Rather than wigwams, they learned to build cabins. Their small community settled as they were progressively subdued. It was as if their wings had been clipped, and they succumbed to their landlocked existence.

Geronimo was soon an old man in his sixties. He was no longer the defiant warrior, and a calmness had come over him. Over the years, he had wed multiple women and fathered several children, but many of them died. Out in the flat lands of Oklahoma, his people were shrinking in numbers.

Scene in Geronimo's camp before the surrender to General Crook. *C.S. Fly, 1886, Library of Congress.*

It surely must have been painful for him to see the little ones reared in a setting removed from their forefathers. There were no canyons to climb, and while the fort contained small rivers, they couldn't compare to the Gila. The younger generation was conflicted in their identities, caught between two cultures and confused about which one to follow. Since they were confined, they experienced a sheltered existence that ended at the border of the reservation. Even Geronimo struggled to retain his beliefs, and after attending abundant Christian sermons, he adopted some of the Christian faith himself.

Nearing the end of his life, he was invited to be a part of the 1904 World's Fair held in St. Louis, Missouri. He was apprehensive to attend, but along with some members of his tribe, they agreed to participate. The fair drew millions of people from throughout the world. It was a seven-month-long extravaganza enveloping 1,200 acres in Forest Park. A section was designated for the Apache to camp but was guarded by military officials. The organizers aimed to highlight different cultures as forms of attractions, and from one perspective, this was enlightening to the spectators. But at the same time, it was rather objectifying for those placed on display.

Geronimo and Apaches at the St. Louis Fair, Missouri, 1904. *Library of Congress.*

To Geronimo's own surprise, he enjoyed the fair immensely. He met people from places he had never heard of before. While he was exposed to others as a type of fascinating exhibit, they were also exposed to him. Performing in the Wild West shows, he showcased his roping skills for applauding crowds. He was intrigued by the magic shows, sword fights, and bears that could walk on their hind legs. Maybe the fair was actually good for his soul, as he described his amusement of taking his first Ferris wheel ride. The fearless Geronimo laughed with his guards over his sudden fear of heights while riding in what he called "the little house" in the sky. When remembering his experience at the fair, it seemed to be one of the few occasions he enjoyed himself in his older age: "I am glad I went to the Fair. I saw many interesting things and learned much of the white people. They are a very kind and peaceful people. During all the time I was at the Fair no one tried to harm me in any way. Had this been among the Mexicans I am sure I should have been compelled to defend myself often. I wish all my people could have attended the Fair."

When Geronimo was asked the following year to march in Theodore Roosevelt's Inaugural Parade, he gladly accepted the invitation. He rode

Above: Indian chiefs headed by Geronimo at President Roosevelt's Inauguration Day, Washington, D.C. *Keystone View Company and B.L. Singley, circa 1905, Library of Congress.*

Right: Geronimo. *Edward S. Curtis, circa 1905, New York Public Library Digital Collections.*

horseback, adorning a headdress of feathers, in unison with five other Indian chiefs from different tribes. Once the parade ended, they were brought to the White House, where he was given a moment to speak to Roosevelt. With only one chance, he begged for the president to allow his return to Arizona. An interpreter relayed his words: "I pray you cut the ropes and make me free. Let me die in my own country, an old man who has been punished long enough and is free." His attempt was met with compassion, but Roosevelt denied his plea.

Approaching the dawn of his eightieth year, Geronimo fell off his horse in Fort Sill and laid throughout the night in pouring rain. As a consequence of this, he became sick with pneumonia. His body was tired and could no longer fight. He died on February 17, 1909, and was buried at the Fort Sill Beef Creek Apache Cemetery, in defiance of his one final wish. As he concluded in his own story, "It is my land, my home, my fathers' land, to which I now ask to be allowed to return. I want to spend my last days there, and be buried among those mountains....[I]f I must die in bondage—I hope that the remnant of the Apache tribe may, when I am gone, be granted the one privilege which they request—to return to Arizona."

If the afterlife exists, as Geronimo believed it did, his spirit would certainly have escaped to the wild of Arizona, where the canyons rise by the headwaters of the Gila River.

The Kachina Woman of Sedona

Raw beauty and mysticism converge in Sedona. It's often considered the jewel of Arizona for these reasons. This small town, with a mix of new age wisdom and old western culture, welcomes visitors from all over the world. Roaming through hundreds of artsy shops, tourists pick up crystals, rocks, and gemstones as souvenirs. Psychics read their palms in rooms tucked behind beaded curtains, where the scent of incense floats amid the candlelight. The more one is immersed in the scene, the more it all begins to make sense. To truly experience Sedona's wonder, the heart has to be open to its magic.

Depending on the time of day, the mountains change color, from crimson and rust to purple at sundown. Paintings on gallery walls in the village of Tlaquepaque showcase the unique views of Sedona's shades. However, beyond the gorgeous scenery, there is a phenomenon here that may *only* be felt. Few places have such a strong connection to vortexes as Sedona. Although they are known to exist in various locations throughout the globe, Sedona is renowned for its collection of these obscure centers of energy.

A vortex is a site of whirling energy originating within the ground and atmosphere. Some people are more sensitive to the effects of a vortex than others. Depending on the individual, one may experience a wide range of feelings in both the spiritual and physical sense. Conflicting accounts regarding the same vortex are common; one person may feel calm, while another becomes invigorated. While there are limited scientific theories regarding the vortexes in Sedona, the enigma has been held sacred even among Arizona's earliest inhabitants.

Just north of town, Boynton Canyon contains one of the most potent of Sedona's four best-known vortexes. It's also the site of Kachina Woman, a tall spire of sandstone rock distinctive in its silhouette by the side of a larger mountain. This formation stands to one side of a plateau that extends outward to a knoll at its farthest edge. While the Kachina Woman keeps high above the valley below, the climb to the plateau is a reasonable grade. When setting out on the trail, the juniper trees are noticeably twisted. Their branches seem to have been in a constant struggle between their desire to naturally grow upward toward the sun against a power pulling them into the ground. It's suggested that the vortex has caused their distortion.

Kachina Woman Mountain, Boynton Canyon, Sedona, Arizona. *Jessica Laughlin.*

Archaeologists believe that the Verde Valley was inhabited by the Paleoindian people roughly fourteen thousand years ago. This group lived throughout the Southwest, and their main source of sustenance was from hunting large animals. Thousands of years passed before the ancient Sinagua people entered the valley and began farming the rich soil along the Verde River. Their presence in Arizona traces to AD 650; however, research suggests that they entered the area of Sedona in about AD 1125. They certainly were impressed by the red rocks, as they literally settled right into them and built remarkable cliff-side dwellings. Montezuma Castle National Monument in Camp Verde, along with the Palatki and Honanki Heritage Sites found northwest of Sedona, are remarkable examples of this prehistoric architecture. These ancient ones are thought to have performed ceremonies and rituals in Boynton Canyon.

Many tribes across Arizona share in having Sinagua blood running through their ancestry, but the Hopi and Zuni believe they are direct ancestors. To the Hopi, the Kachina Woman has been a symbol of the female essence since antiquity and protects all of the Kachinas. Kachinas are spirit guides with diverse personalities meant to assist the Pueblo people throughout life. Some Kachinas personify the animal world, such as Crow Mother, White Bear, and the Buffalo Warrior. Although they are invisible, they serve as a connection between mortals and the gods. The Hopi began to make Kachina dolls to educate their young about their mythology. The creation of these dolls was followed by the Navajo, Zuni, and other tribes who incorporated them into their own cultures.

Similar to the vortex, the power of the Kachinas may only be felt by those willing to open themselves to the spiritual realm. This same majestic canyon is likewise sacred to the Yavapai and Apache, who call it "Che Ah Chi," translating to "red rocks." According to Yavapai lore, it's where the first woman gave birth. This could explain why some come here to elevate their connection to Mother Earth and have received profound clarity. Along with creation stories rooted in the area, the Yavapai have their own form of spiritual guides called the "Kakaka." These small but mighty beings live in the mountains, including Boynton Canyon. They taught their people how to live well in the beginning and also showed them how to dance the Kakaka Iima, the "Mountain Spirit Dance."

All of these legends are connected to Boynton Canyon and its defender, the Kachina Woman. On clear and bright afternoons, standing against her imposing side, one can see for miles across a terrain of bedrock speckled with greenery. Crows glide against the sky, keeping watch, for they are the

The Kachinas. *Jessica Laughlin.*

messengers of Mother Earth. Everything here is alive, even the funnels of swirling energy seeping in and out of the earth's ground like a form of respiration. Kachina Woman has watched over every raindrop and each new sprout of life. She has seen the inauguration of many civilizations, but while they have come and gone, the rocks hold their stories.

NATIVE AND URBAN LEGENDS: THE MOGOLLON MONSTER AND NAVAJO SKINWALKERS

Lurking in the shadows of Arizona's buttes and forests, dread tales emanate from the backcountry. The nights are often illuminated only by the brilliant moon and stars. By the firelight of campsites, stories about Navajo Skinwalkers and the Mogollon Monster have been passed down for generations. Told in whispers, the storyteller pauses as he dramatically builds anticipation. Then, as if on cue, a pinecone falls from a branch, and his audience gasps before breaking into laughter. Yet apart from their thrill of a scare, maybe these are not just myths of the woods. For the unlucky ones who've encountered these creatures, they hold them to be true. The trepidation remains on their faces and embeds in their souls. It is possible that despite all mankind knows, there are still things that are unexplainable.

The Navajos have long lived near Monument Valley in the northeastern corner of Arizona. Their buttes are like natural cathedrals rising. Depending on the weather, the mood of their land fluctuates often. Before a storm, clouds drift over the looming peaks, and their formations often appear as apparitions in the darkened sky. Along with the dramatic landscape, the valley is also the site of many supernatural narratives, including those of Skinwalkers. These shapeshifting demons have been observed by the Navajo and others for eons. Their diabolic spirits emerge unexpectedly and are perceived as a bad omen. Danger and illness can strike anyone who witnesses one of these beasts. According to their folklore, they are humans who made an unforgiveable pact, trading their souls to the evil spirits for immortality. As witches, they are able to transform into various animals like bears, coyotes, or werewolves. Their presence in Arizona has brought about both curiosity and terror.

South of Navajo country, along the Mogollon Rim, the forests are thick and wooded. The rim is defined by cragged rocks and cliffs overlooking the Coconino National Forest. From the vantage point of its fringe, evergreens blanket the earth for as far as one can see. It's easy to assume that some of this forested land has seldom been touched by mankind. This leads to a question: Could it be possible that a beast has managed to hide within the thicket, concealing himself from the outside world? Well, anything is plausible, especially when bearing in mind the remoteness of the region.

Similar to Bigfoot, the Mogollon Monster is a primitive combination of man and ape. His face is hairless, but his body is covered in fur. He walks

Coyote in the desert. *Jessica Laughlin.*

upright, albeit hunched over at the shoulders, and is taller than an average man. For more than a century, people have claimed to see the monster in the Mogollon Rim and Grand Canyon. Accounts from scared witnesses are ample. Of course, numerous testaments are merely the product of overactive minds, and a bear could easily be mistaken for the monster. Some terrifying accounts, however, are convincing. Whether these cryptic beings are out there, hiding in Arizona's forlorn places, remains shrouded in myth—but this could be for the best.

The Hohokam Canal People of Phoenix

Where there is water, there is life. Although the Sonoran Desert has less of this precious resource, nature has provided enough for it to flourish in its own way. The saguaro cacti, prickly pears, and brittle brush are havens for wildlife that make their homes in this climate. One of the cleverest inhabitants is the cactus wren, a petite bird that builds its nests inside the native cacti. By doing so, they fend off their predators, as the sharp spines make it impossible for even a coyote to forage. They also receive most of their water from a diet primarily consisting of bugs and cacti flowers, eliminating the need to quench their thirst. Each day brings challenges to the wise animals that live in this region, but they have learned to adapt.

Frankly, survival for all species in this desert has grim odds, but the forms of life here became experts in defying its obstacles. This is apparent in Arizona's largest cities, Phoenix and Tucson. Their unexpected growth, coupled with the Southwest's dwindling water supply, has brought about an urgent call for innovative water management. In spite of the concern of the tap running dry, mankind seems up for the challenge against the desert. This is why most people residing here have done away with their grassy lawns, choosing desert landscaping instead. However, watering grass is only one of several factors contributing to the problematic situation.

Since ancient times, the Sonoran Desert has endured periods of substantial rainfall and severe drought. Those who lived in the region as early as two thousand years ago also grappled in the quest for water security. Of all the early people who seasonally migrated through the Phoenix and Tucson areas, the Hohokam were the first to establish widespread irrigational communities. Historians broadly agree that their timeframe in the Salt and Gila River Basins began around AD 1 and concluded sometime

The Hohokam canal people. *Jessica Laughlin.*

near AD 1450. Different theories have been implied as to why their thriving population vanished, but it's held that they are the ancestors of the O'odham and Pima. Their namesake, "Hohokam," translates to "exhausted" and "the people who have gone."

It could have been that they were exhausted from the desert's repressive heat and water woes, or possibly it was the result of another catastrophe. Whatever the case, their villages were left to disintegrate in the scorching sun, although pieces from their culture and proof of their prosperous society still remain. One of these relics is the Great House of Casa Grande Ruins National Monument, southeast of Phoenix in Coolidge. The structure on a barren field is just a section of the original. For being one of the oldest prehistoric buildings in America, it's frequently overlooked. Hohokam compounds surrounded individual homes that were built close together, much like the walls encompassing our subdivisions. They also included plazas and ball courts that were similar to modern sporting venues. Using caliche—made of clay, sand, and calcium carbonate—these buildings were well insulated against the summer heat.

Needless to say, the Hohokam were an advanced society. They wove intricate baskets and designed jewelry not only from materials found in their immediate region but also from those they received through trade partners in present-day Mexico. Their agricultural communities thrived for centuries because of their ingenuity in creating complex canal systems to irrigate their crops. As engineering masters, they diverted water from two primary rivers, the Salt and Gila, allowing their villages to expand away from the riverside and farther into the valley. Without the luxury of machines, they used only simple tools to dig hundreds of miles of interweaving canals. With more food and access to water, all Hohokam reaped the benefits, and the population swelled. Archaeologists maintain that tens of thousands Hohokam people lived in the valley.

Imagine fields of corn, beans, and squash harvested in the exact same locations where shopping centers, buildings, and freeways stand now. All of this is owed to the Hohokam intellect and their canals, which still weave through the city of Phoenix like veins, supplying the lifeblood for a metropolis. When the Hohokam abandoned the area, the network of waterways began to dry out and became nothing more than ditches plugged with debris. The canals required care and maintenance to keep the water flowing, which ceased after their mysterious departure. The potential of the canals wouldn't be realized again until 1867 by prospector Jack Swilling.

When Swilling noticed the parched canals, he was living in nearby Wickenburg. With an entrepreneurial personality, he was constantly on the move when it came to financial endeavors. Throughout his lifetime, he had a host of careers. It's been recorded that he was a military man, rancher, miner, postal express rider, saloon owner, and much more. For a brilliant man, he also had addictions that caused him trouble. Opiates and alcohol were used to dull the pain of a fractured skull he received from being hit over the head by a revolver, and a bullet somehow remained lodged in his side. It's not surprising that a man of his character would be the one to see promise in an empty desert valley, as the West was practically settled by the determination of wayward dreamers. They were the ones who saw glimmers of gold where others just saw dirt. When Swilling happened upon the canals, he immediately knew that they were meant for irrigation.

He founded the Swilling Irrigating and Canal Company and then set out to revitalize the canals. A post office was established in 1868, and Swilling served as postmaster. Phoenix was named for its symbolic connection to the Greek Phoenix, a bird that rises from the ashes of the past. As the name implies, Phoenix rose from the dust of the canals built by the Hohokam people. While the capital of the Arizona Territory was then Prescott, it was changed to Phoenix in 1889. The influx of pioneers to the area was cause for the conversion, and from that point forward, Phoenix has been one of the fastest-growing cities in the Southwest. We have to wonder if the population of the Hohokam eventually overwhelmed their water supply, causing a condition similar to our current problem.

The canals have undergone numerous restorations since they were initially dug by the Hohokam. They are lined with concrete, and only a minuscule portion of the canals have been preserved in their archaic state. Cutting through neighborhoods and central city streets, they have become discreet observers of change. Along with the Colorado River, the water diverted from the Salt River through the canals continues to be a primary water source for the "Valley of the Sun." As the Southwest foresees a future of water uncertainty, the principles of cooperation that were vital to the Hohokam are similarly relevant in our times. As the water flows tenderly through Phoenix, in some ways, the Hohokam live on through the gift of their canals.

Old Bill Williams, the Mountain Man

William Sherley Williams usually appears in western yore as "Old Bill, the Mountain Man" or "Old Solitaire," but Bill was a rogue adventurer well before his beard turned gray. He was one of the first mountain men to live with Native tribes and brave the country most men of his time would never lay eyes on. Although he was born in 1787 in Polk County, North Carolina, his family migrated to St. Louis, Missouri, when he was just a lad. As a boy, he was religious, and to his parents' pride, he became a Baptist preacher at only seventeen. He joined a group of traveling Baptist missionaries who were heading into Osage country in Missouri. Their intention was to share the teachings of Christianity with the tribe. During his time among the Osage, he took enough of a liking to their people that he essentially deserted his own prior ways entirely. By all indications, rather than converting them, he was enlightened instead.

Williams determined that the path he had previously been heading down was not leading to the future he had in mind. Most of his peers likely couldn't understand his desire to begin anew with the Natives, but he was a headstrong individual who didn't bend easily to the will of others. While in the company of the Osage, he became skilled in hunting bison. He began to dress in their manner, wearing clothing made of buckskins. His reddish hair grew long, and he didn't shave. Out in the wild, there were no state lines, and he kept venturing farther into territories outside of U.S. control.

Bill Williams, the mountain man. *Jessica Laughlin.*

His independence was a quality that would define the mountain man for years to come.

Because of his knowledge of the Osage language, he assisted in creating an Osage English dictionary of phrases and words. He also served as an interpreter during the War of 1812. For a while, he worked as a surveyor of the Santa Fe Trail. Williams possessed a calmness in his demeanor, and therefore he was accepted by Indigenous people, who sensed that his intentions were in the right place. He helped define the route of the trail by working with the tribes in a diplomatic way. Pieces of his life story are sewn together as a patched quilt, and we have only tattered remnants. Nonetheless, it's easy to gather from most accounts that he was humble and genuinely respected Native societies.

In his twenties, Williams married an Osage woman named A-Ci'n-Ga. She died after the birth of their second daughter though, leaving Williams with limited options to care for them. Not much is known about the girls' upbringing, but they were sent to a boarding school in Kentucky and never knew their father very well. The solitude of the wilderness may have been his only comfort, as he would leave for months at a time into the frontier.

He rode through blond grasslands covering the plains, their blades softly whispering with each gust of wind. The prairies waved beneath skies of drifting clouds. When a silence came upon the landscape, it was broken by a colossal rumble of bison in all their glory, hundreds in a single herd, pounding their weight into the ground as they ran in unison. From the flat plains, Williams forged into the Rockies, where impenetrable snowcapped mountain chains were contrasted by delicate wildflowers gracing the spring hillsides below. In his daring escapades, he came across bears, elk, and deer, each uneasily aware of the other. He navigated the perennial streams and through groves of aspens like a wild creature himself.

He hunted and traded with Native people, acquainting himself with their tribes in the process. West of Missouri, many of them hadn't encountered a white man before, but most were welcoming. He would return east and on occasion find work as a scout guiding others into the frontier. To put the timeline in perspective within the broader context, Williams was exploring the continent while Kit Carson was a kid, and it's likely that their paths may have crossed when Carson worked as a saddlemaker in Franklin, Missouri. Williams was a rare breed of original fur trapper, endearing himself to the next generation, who gave him the nickname "Old Bill."

It's believed that during his most active years, he journeyed into the woodlands of northern Arizona. He may have been accompanied by other trappers, or he could have been alone. The forests encompassed huge distances where one could get lost and never return. Williams was the kind who enjoyed solitude, though, so this land must have attracted him. Numerous waterways in timbered seclusion were prime for hunting beaver, whose furs had become a valuable commodity back east. He roamed these woods, shaded by canopies of ponderosa pines.

Here and there he ventured, never establishing a permanent home on record anywhere. Sometimes his nomadic wanderings traced to New Mexico, where he possibly wintered near Taos, and he also frequented Bent's Fort on the Santa Fe Trail. Because of his notoriety, when Kit Carson wasn't available for John C. Frémont's fourth expedition to Colorado in 1848, Frémont hired Williams to lead his party. They had connected at Bent's Fort, and Williams agreed to the offer. Unfortunately, they embarked on the mission too late in the year, facing a fury of snowstorms and below-freezing temperatures. In the miserable frost, many of their mules and horses died, alongside men who starved and froze to death. It's been stated that Frémont was determined to cross the Rocky Mountains despite warnings by Williams and others that the conditions were too dangerous. By the end of their fatal voyage, dozens of men had succumbed. This was damaging to Frémont's celebrated reputation—he placed the blame on Williams.

As Williams was a man of warm character who rarely kept an enemy, it could be assumed that the loss of these men distressed his conscience. The remainder of his life isn't well documented because he probably retreated again into the solace of nature until he met his death in 1849 in the southwestern pocket of Colorado. Ute warriors are said to have mistaken his identity and accidentally killed him. Claims were made that after realizing it was Williams, they respectfully buried his body by the banks of a river. If there was a place Williams would have wanted to rest, it would likely have been somewhere like this, in the lonely spaces between mountain ranges.

In 1881, the town of Williams, Arizona, was founded and named in his honor. For more than a century, it's been a resting place for travelers on the open road. Developed around the railroad, it became the depot for steam locomotive train rides to the South Rim of the Grand Canyon. Then in 1926, Route 66 led road-trippers directly through its main street of neon signs, shops, and motels. As Route 66 evolved into America's melting pot of culture and coolness, Williams lived up to this essence. When the highway eventually bypassed town and the prime era of the Mother Road reached an end, the town leaned further into being the "Gateway to the Grand Canyon" and continued to welcome tourists.

In Williams, the past remains blended with the new. Those retro signs still glow in the evenings along the thoroughfare, bringing us back in time to when cross-country road trips were a rite of passage. Dating even further back, the brick buildings that once were brothels and saloons are now the sites of bars and restaurants. Travelers from across the world stay in Williams when visiting the Grand Canyon, seeing a side of America's charm at the foothills of picturesque mountains. Truckers and long-haul road warriors alike stop in at the local diner in the pines for home-cooked meals and huge slices of crème pie. Then they stroll by the statue of Bill Williams, the elusive trailblazer, the wanderer of old, a man who, like the town, forever represents the adventurous spirit of America.

The Captivity of Olive and Mary Ann Oatman

There are few portraits of Olive Oatman, but those that exist are captivating. The prominent lines on her chin and solemn stare in her eyes reveal only the surface of a dreadful yet harrowing story. She was one of seven children. Her parents, Royse and Mary Ann, were once farmers and owners of a successful mercantile business in La Harpe, Illinois. The country was prospering in the 1830s, and so were the Oatmans, at least for a while. This was until a downturn in the financial markets trickled downstream from the banks to American families around 1842. The Oatmans' store shelves grew bare, prices of goods became too low, and soon enough they were closing their doors. The succeeding period in their lives was latent with despair, but they tried to remain optimistic. Royse was the kind of man who held an unshakable positivity and refused to give in to the tough times. The family relocated to the Cumberland Valley in Pennsylvania, but after realizing that this didn't appeal to them, they returned to Illinois. Disheartened but not broken, they settled in a small cabin located near Fulton, amid prairies of tall grass dotted with blooms and other farms.

In this rural Illinois farming community, they were drawn to the beliefs of the Latter-day Saints. They converted from Methodism to Mormonism, finding virtue written in the prophecies of founder Joseph Smith. They became faithful followers of the Book of Mormon, and the passages helped them through their hardships. All the while, there was growing dissention toward the church spreading throughout the region. This anger, stemming from judgment, surfaced when Joseph Smith and his brother were violently killed in 1844 by a mob while jailed for alleged treason in Carthage, Illinois. Smith's murder rattled the Mormon Church, and his followers were in a state of disarray as to who would succeed in his role. As an apostle of Smith, Brigham Young rose to be prophet and at once began preparing for their exodus to Utah. The church gained momentum under his leadership, but the Oatmans didn't agree with some of his actions and interpretations of the scripture. While hundreds followed Young to the Great Salt Lake Valley, arriving

Olive Oatman. *Jessica Laughlin.*

there in 1847, the Oatmans untangled their ties to the core congregation and began following another Mormon leader, James Brewster.

Brewster differed from Young and didn't see the Salt Lake Valley as their holy Zion. He claimed that the rightful settlement for their church should be near the Gila River on the border between Arizona and California. He referred to this region as "Bashan" and the followers of his faction became Brewsterites. Feasibly, something about this speck of optimism stirred the tides within Royse and Mary Ann. Now in their thirties, the thought of running away from the mundane likely brought needed respite to their tired souls. They were revived as a couple, suddenly elated as if all the baggage they had between them could be forgotten. Not only was Brewster pushing the move for religious reasons, but the United States government was also encouraging settlers to migrate to the Southwest. The horizon beyond appeared idyllic, where the weather was mild and families could fare well in farming. With this perfect vision in sight, they eagerly packed what they could bring and sold the rest. They signed up to be one of the families to join Brewster's wagon party west, which consisted of ninety people and twenty-seven wagons. This would be the Oatmans' final farewell to Illinois, but the road ahead looked brighter.

They joined the others following Brewster in Independence, Missouri, on August 9, 1850, and headed into the Southwest by way of the Santa Fe Trail. Their wagons were well stocked with provisions; their cattle and horses were buoyant as they began. The Oatmans, huddled together, were as enthusiastic as the others. Their spirited exhilaration seemed to wrap around their wagon party as a halo, where nothing bad could fall on them. The skies were clear and the air crisp, and there was nothing but open land. They were off on an adventure, and one can imagine that it had been a while since the couple had felt this kind of happiness.

The kinship between the families was strong. They were all ready to contribute to the common good. As twilight fell on the fields and the sun retreated, they stopped to camp for the evening. Each individual partook in hitching the tents and making up the campsite for an evening of rest. Hot meals were prepared over open flames, and as they relaxed, they got to know their new friends better. Refreshed by the light of day, they loaded their supplies to begin again.

A long journey, no matter how strong a person may be, takes a toll on the body. Tiredness sets in, sickness follows, and irritability breeds. This started to happen among the Brewsterites as one day melted into the next. The dust of the dirty path covered their belongings and seeped into their

The Oatman family in their wagon. *Jessica Laughlin.*

pores. Moods took a turn, including that of Brewster himself. Seeds of disagreements and nuisances were planted among the party as their supplies became more limited with every passing mile. Their oxen were also showing signs of exhaustion from the load they had pulled across the nothingness. The glimmer was fading.

Some in their wagon party changed course about halfway through New Mexico. At a fork in the route, they had a choice of taking one of two paths. This became a heated debate among them, essentially dividing the party in two. The Oatmans, among other like-minded families, felt that it was best to head south through Socorro and then cross by way of the southwestern pass to Tucson. The result was an observable vulnerability in traveling with fewer people and supplies. There were also frequent, startling encounters with some Native groups along the way. In *The Captivity of the Oatman Girls*, Lorenzo, the eldest brother, recalled their constant anxiety: "One morning three large, fierce looking Apaches came into camp at an early hour. They put on all possible pretensions of friendship; but from the first, their movements were suspicious. They for a time surveyed narrowly our wagons and our teams, and, so far as allowed to do so, our articles of food, clothing, guns, etc. Suspecting their intentions we bade them be off, upon which they reluctantly left our retreat. That night the dogs kept up a barking nearly the whole night, and at seasons of the night would run to their masters, and then a short distance into the wood, as if to warn us of the nearness of danger." According to Lorenzo, the next morning some livestock were gone, leaving them even more susceptible to hazards.

As they trudged onward, contouring the Rio Grande, a longing for home in Illinois surely was on all of their minds. This wasn't the promised land they had envisioned, nor was the trail close to what they thought it would be. At this point, presumably, Royse was beyond reason, as he had nothing in Illinois, and the zest for the journey was gone. It must have hit as a cruel reality against those intoxicating dreams. How many pioneers had come before him, impassioned at first but then consumed by regret far into the trail of painstaking hardship? After an arduous trek over mountains and rivers, most among the dwindled party were relieved to see signs of other human life, stopping in Tucson. The Oatmans and two other families kept going on to Maricopa Wells, and upon finding the Indians of the Pimo (Pima) Village to be kindhearted, they decided to stay for a while in the vicinity. After meeting a Dr. Lecount, who had just returned from Fort Yuma, affirming that he had encountered no difficulties in between, Royse resolved that they were too close to their final destination to give up. Fort Yuma was roughly two hundred miles to the west, and although they were unaccompanied, they chose to push ahead.

Several days later, on his return to Fort Yuma, Dr. Lecount, in the company of a Mexican guide, found the destitute family again. They were famished and fighting the terrain. He assured them that he would head straight to the fort to gather assistance, but the army's help did not arrive in time to save them. They underestimated the real danger in this war-torn territory, whose conflicts had been raging for centuries among the Native tribes, Spanish, and Mexicans. They couldn't possibly have grasped the dynamics of this beaten and bloodied place. It was a new part of America with *very old* hostilities. The wounds from ancient times were still bleeding. Venomous resentments were bred from stolen lives and land. It was a merciless stretch of desolation that this lone family found themselves innocently walking across, as gentle as sheep. They assumed that they would be unharmed, and in this naivete, they were doomed. Further complicating the region's age-old battles was the recently ended Mexican-American War.

In the faraway cliffs, eyes had been stalking them for miles. Crouched low behind their shields of imperfect rocks, a group of Native men observed the Oatmans struggle against the disorientating desert's blinding rays and heat. Without warning, they appeared in their midst like ghosts. Even in infancy, the Oatmans' baby must have recognized the tears forming in his mother's eyes at their approach—an encounter that her intuition may have warned would be coming. But still, they had continued, and now this was the outcome. They asked for items and food, of which Royse asserted they had too little to spare, but he gave them tobacco and some scraps of bread. When denied their request for more, their demeanor changed abruptly. A brutal massacre followed with the use of blades and stone clubs.

In Olive's own words:

> *As they had taken me oneside, and while one of the Indians was leading me off, I saw them strike Lorenzo, and, almost at the same instant, my father also. I was so bewildered and taken by surprise by the suddenness of their movements, and their deafening yells, that it was some little time before I could realize the horrors of my situation. When I turned around, opened my eyes, and collected my thoughts, I saw my father, my own dear father! struggling, bleeding, and moaning in the most pitiful manner. Lorenzo was lying with his face in the dust, the top of his head covered with blood, and his ears and mouth bleeding profusely. I looked around and saw my poor mother, with her youngest child clasped in her arms, and both of them still, as if the work of death had already been completed; a little distance on the opposite side of the wagon, stood little Mary Ann, with her face covered with her hands, sobbing aloud, and a huge looking Indian standing over her; the rest were motionless, save a younger brother and my father,—all upon the ground dead or dying.*

Her mother and father, along with four of her siblings, were slaughtered. The children ranged in age from one to seventeen. Olive's brother Lorenzo was so callously struck that he was considered by Olive to be dead. Olive, fourteen, and her younger sister Mary Ann, only eight, were then taken as slaves. After being in a state of unconsciousness for an unknown length of time, Lorenzo awoke to a most disturbing realization. Partially scalped, holding his bleeding head, he stumbled to rise. Blood was dried on his forehead, and gasping of thirst and in agonizing disbelief, he discovered that his sisters were gone and the remainder of his family were slain. The type of pain he endured is incomprehensible. He paced through the vastness, almost dead, for days before he was discovered by the Pima. They sympathetically nurtured his wounds, giving him food and shelter. On their way back to the village, the two families who had remained behind in Maricopa Wells were now on the same route they had traveled. At the sight of Lorenzo, they tried to console his tortured soul. He rode back with them to the site of the massacre and then on to Fort Yuma to seek help.

Lorenzo spent the following years pleading with others for assistance in finding his sisters. This was thought to be a futile effort, as the general assumption was that his sisters were deceased. However, for more than a year after the massacre, the enslaved Olive and Mary Ann were very much alive, living through hard labor, meager rations, and frequent beatings. Their treatment was devoid of humanity, and they often conveyed their desire to die. In her later chronicles, she stated that her captors were "Touto Apaches" (Tonto), but this has been historically contested; it could have been a faction of the Yavapai. In a fateful turn of events, this tribe met with the Mojave to trade. Like cattle at auction, they were exchanged for supplies.

Now in the care of the Mojave, they were brought to their village, situated along the banks of the Colorado River. Their lands were like an oasis in the desert, different from where they were before. They were also treated with some respect and adapted slightly to the Mojaves' customs, but they never fully assimilated. Notably, in Olive's narrative, the chief's daughter, Topeka, showed the most affection toward their welfare. Although the conditions were comparably better, the sisters were still enslaved and considered property. The difference was that the girls weren't mistreated physically, and over time, they felt safer within the community. Bonds were formed, and although there were instances of tenderness toward them, they were regarded as captives, not as equals.

After living with the Mojave for some time, the Oatmans were required to have their faces tattooed by a medicine man. It was common for the Mojave to give their people tattoos for the sake of identification among other tribes and in the afterlife. Using a sharp stick, juice from a weed, and powder from a blue stone, the man drew multiple lines on their chins. As if life couldn't get any harder for these girls, the tribe entered a severe famine for an extended duration. Their soils produced minimal crops, leaving the entire village malnourished. They ate whatever morsels and berries they could find. Mary Ann, who was already frail and too weak to survive, died from sickness brought on by starvation. Every effort Olive made to keep her sister alive failed her in the end. Without her sister by her side, she was lonelier than ever before. The Mojave were notably compassionate toward her during this time, making an allowance for her to bury her sister instead of their custom of cremation.

Although she thought about finding a way to escape, she feared for her life if she tried. This feeling was renewed when, after a brief engagement of war with the Cocopah, the Mojave claimed victory and brought back captives from their tribe. One of the taken souls was a woman whom Olive found to be particularly beautiful. She was a mother, heartsick over the distance from her two-year-old child. She attempted to flee by swimming down the Colorado River and hiding under the mesquite trees, but when she was caught, the result was a slow death while she was nailed upright to a stake. Regardless of the relationships Olive formed among the tribe, this instance of cruelty to another captive reignited traumas from her past.

When Olive was nineteen, soldiers from Fort Yuma received information that led them to believe she was living with the Mojave. This came as a surprise to Lorenzo, who had been despairingly searching for more than five years. A Yuma messenger by the name of Francisco brought a dire warning to the village that the military would soon arrive. The chief and others met for a council to decide how to proceed, and an uproar of commotion was heard throughout the camp. Olive was overcome by suspense and the possibility of freedom. She also feared being killed instead. Francisco pleaded and asserted that if they chose to not release her, the fury of the United States would fall on the backs of not only the Mojave but the Yuma as well.

After many days of weighing the risks, a chief concluded that Olive would be set free. An uncontrollable happiness came over her, and she later reflected, "While yet in their presence, I found I could no longer control my feelings, and I burst into tears, no longer able to deny myself the pleasure of thus expressing the weight of feeling that struggled for relief and utterance within me." The hardest part of leaving the village was parting forever with her dear sister, who would remain in the soil of a land so far from home.

It was arranged for her to be accompanied by Francisco and some Yuma men to Fort Yuma. Topeka bravely volunteered to join her on the ride back. She genuinely felt saddened by the parting, and it was perhaps Topeka who was behind the sparing of her life. When they finally arrived at the fort on February 28, 1856, a cheering and exhilarated crowd awaited. Topeka was given a horse by the military as a sign of good will. Soon afterward, Olive's brother made his way to the fort. She was stunned to learn that he was alive, as she had thought for five years that he had been killed. With tears in their eyes and immense emotion, they were at last reunited. Although they were

Right: Portrait of Olive Oatman. *Benjamin F. Powelson, circa 1860s, National Gallery of Art.*

Below: A sign on a restaurant in Oatman, Arizona. *Author's collection.*

scarred mentally and physically, they once again had the spark of hope that they remembered from their father's eyes.

When news of her survival hit the press, it captured national attention. Books were written about her story, her face was printed on souvenir cards, and she toured the country with her brother. Although she tried to integrate into conventional society, she struggled with her identity thereafter. Understandably, she was haunted by the massacre and likely spent many nights awake reliving the terrifying events. As a resilient survivor, Olive experienced some happiness in her life when she found love, marrying a rancher named John Fairchild. They lived a quiet life, settling in the countryside of Sherman, Texas. They also adopted an infant girl who was named Mary, after her mother and sister. She gave it her all to overcome the heartbreak, but Olive was emotionally traumatized. The tattoo on her chin was also a constant reminder of her inner anguish. Although she was a free woman, a part of her may have always been a captive girl. She oftentimes wore a veil to conceal her face and became withdrawn in her older age, passing away in 1903 at sixty-five.

The town of Oatman, Arizona, deep in the Black Mountains east of Bullhead City, was named after Olive in 1909. Because of its proximity to where she lived with the Mojave, she could have traversed this very location while in captivity. It is perhaps best known for its roaming burros and Wild West character. When gold was discovered in the early 1900s, miners flocked to the area, and a town rose out of the dirt. As one of the quirkiest living ghost towns, it became a popular stop along the way to California on Route 66. When the road was redirected, Oatman went through difficult times, but it persevered, just like the brave woman for whom it was named.

Prescott's Infamous Whiskey Row

Let's return for a moment to the height of Montezuma Street in Prescott, back when the roads were a mess of mud. There we'd see fogged windows and the iridescence of low-lit, crowded saloons, filled to the brim with winners, losers, and troublemakers. Enclosed behind the swinging wooden doors, we would find rows of poker tables with every seat taken. A sea of hats and parlor girl feathers floated here and there. The smoky air masked the aroma of spilled booze, sweat, cigarettes, and stale perfume, and a pianist would be over in the corner, sitting politely on his bench. He was a contradiction among the crowd, wearing his best suit and bowtie, mustache swirled, thin fingers moving about the keys. He kept the tune jolly, merrily drowning out the cussing, hollers, laughter, broken glasses, and brawls. This was Whiskey Row in the late 1800s, where the music bellowed down the block from roughly forty bars, all tightly packed together in a huddle of debauchery. Here, in this imagined scene of old, the night was young and tomorrow didn't matter all that much.

Whiskey Row in Prescott was one of the most scandalous blocks in Arizona's wildest days of yore. Prescott began as a mining camp after gold deposits were found there in 1863. The granite mountains throughout the area proved to also contain an extensive array of minerals and gemstones.

Whiskey Row. *Jessica Laughlin.*

Exterior view of the courthouse in Prescott, Arizona, circa 1890–1920. *USC Libraries and California Historical Society.*

Once it became clear that the town was destined to grow, it was designated as the territorial capital of Arizona one year later. Prescott possessed a blend of people who had come from all walks of life. Members of high society, miners, and cowboys cohabitated as neighbors. With minimal establishments, saloons were the life breath of the frontier, where everyone could gather at the confluence of whiskey and beer. Naturally, they could all too quickly become unpredictable, especially when the wrong two gunslingers had a few too many drinks.

The first courthouse was completed in 1878, and it was a fine, two-story building of brick topped by a clock tower. It was centered in a perfectly square plaza. The courthouse was an enviable centerpiece for the new territory, but coincidentally (or not), it sat directly facing what had already become justly nicknamed "Whiskey Row." Such was life in the old Southwest—law and order on one side and total immorality on the other. Of all the saloons, there was one that stood out among the rest as a favored watering hole. To this day, the Palace Restaurant and Saloon is prized as the oldest bar in the state.

In its earliest years, the Palace was a lively casino where games of faro, poker, and craps were played all day long. It's been rumored that Doc Holliday, who was a skilled poker player, actually won $10,000 here. Careening miners enjoyed the company of the singing saloon dancers. They also served Chinese food along with American dishes, and if one needed a quick haircut, a barbershop was conveniently located in the Palace as well. Among the clinking glassware of this lively place was an exquisite Brunswick bar of hand-carved oak. This sophisticated piece had been shipped by boat and then hauled by mule train to Prescott. Something about its novelty added a touch of class and gave a nod to polite society.

On the evening of July 14, 1900, an unattended candle at a hotel ignited a fire that spread rapidly throughout downtown. Fueled by the dry wooden buildings, it jumped from one to the next, consuming almost all that lay in its path. As the flames grew out of control and the air thickened, over at the Palace, a group of hardened patrons weren't about to allow their adored bar to perish. If they risked their lives in the process, so be it. They rolled up their sleeves and lifted the giant bar with all the strength they had between them. It was brought to safety across the street in the plaza. They also made time to salvage the liquor, of course, and as the town burned down around them, they toasted their efforts. A ferocious fire couldn't dampen the spirits of this crowd. The following morning, the bar stood unscathed amid the smoldering ashes. Fortunately, not a soul died in the fire, but the rest of the Palace burned to the ground. In true pioneering fashion, they tethered their tents right there on the plaza and started to rebuild. One year later, the Palace opened its doors again, transformed into even more of a stunner than before.

This bar sure knows a thing or two, and it certainly would have stories to tell if it could. Other than normal wears of time, minor scratches on its smooth surface, it continues to be a polished beauty for its age. The same bar, in the same place, exists today and is a cherished part of local history. The people whose faces once reflected in the mirrored bar back have since receded into still portraits in gilded frames covering the walls. At night, with music drifting onto the street, cowboys still twirl their honeys. Their boots creak against the wooden floorboards just as they have since the start. The party never ends here on Whiskey Row.

Wickedly Wild Jerome

Ascending a narrow road and hugging a sloping hillside, the drive to Jerome is not for the faint of heart. The steep incline of switchbacks leads to a distinctive town sitting about a mile high over the Verde Valley. Directly underneath the streets packed with Victorian houses and structures from bygone days, more than eighty miles of tunnels once churned out an incredible amount of copper. While it's not a complete ghost town, the current population of several hundred doesn't compare to the fifteen thousand people who resided here at the dawn of the twentieth century.

Halfway between Prescott and Sedona, copper was discovered within the hillside in 1876, but Jerome was officially incorporated in 1899. Likewise, copper turned Bisbee, Arizona, into a thriving city in the 1880s, so everyone assumed that there could be a chance of another boom. As soon as word spread, opportunists moved in, looking for their share. Arriving on the heels of the excitement was the provocative Madame Jennie Bauters. She

Jerome, Arizona. *Jessica Laughlin.*

emigrated from Belgium and headed to Jerome by herself. After settling in the area, she built a two-story building with a wraparound balcony and porch in 1898. It was technically a boardinghouse for women, but this was a façade. Jennie's Place became the heart of the red-light district, and she was soon the wealthiest woman in the territory. Although her building burned down twice in fires, business was simply too good, so she just rebuilt.

Because of its indulgence, Jerome's moniker became the "Wickedest Town in the West." During its peak of deviance, the brothels, saloons, and opium dens provided miners with an escape. When the bell rang out for their shift change, they hit the streets ready to forget their troubles. Because of this, brothels were as essential to mining towns as general stores. Women often became prostitutes because they had no other means to support themselves financially. As Jerome reformed from just a mining camp into a more civilized place with wives and children, there was a change in the tolerance for open prostitution. After a law was enacted in 1913 outlawing brothels downtown, they relocated to Hull Avenue. This was one street below, where a back alleyway connected downtown to the red-light district. It was dubbed "Husband's Alley."

The Southwest is full of colorful towns, but undoubtedly Jerome is among the most vibrant for its history. Coupled with a shady past, many deaths occurred here due to fires, mining accidents, and murders. All of these have turned Jerome into a destination for paranormal investigations. When the shops close their doors at dusk, the streets become eerily silent. Its isolation adds to the chilling ambiance, and for those in tune to ghostly spirits, it's abounding with activity. One of the most haunted sites is the Jerome Grand Hotel. It was once a hospital, so one can presume the type of restless spirits that may wander through the hallways.

Although the nighttime is prime for ghost hunting, there are also frightening places to see during the day. At the Audrey Headframe Park, visitors can walk on a transparent cover directly above a staggering 1,900-foot drop into a mine shaft. The vision of falling—to say nothing of an awakened sense of vertigo—is enough material for nightmares. Aside from the ethereal, it's also fascinating to think of the miners' lives when staring into this void. They lived on the edge, quite literally in Jerome, and spent their working hours in tight and dark spaces below the surface. Embarking into the shaft always held an uncertainty of whether they would see the light again.

Amid countless oddities, the Sliding Jail is the most ironic. Of all the buildings to slip off the precarious mountainside, what are the chances that

Saloon girl. *Jessica Laughlin.*

it would be the jail? Sometime in the 1930s, after too many dynamite blasts at the mines, the jail shimmied off its foundation. It slowly descended until it reached a street 225 feet lower than where it originally stood. Throughout the downhill creep, it remained almost completely intact, eventually landing upright in the middle of Hull Avenue. As unbelievable as this saga may seem already, with Hull Avenue's infamy as the once hot red-light district, it had to be the devious machinations of an outlaw spirit—and one with a wicked sense of humor to boot.

The Lost Dutchman Gold Mine

Out in the desert east of Phoenix, where the cacti thrive and signs of man are rare, there hides a lost treasure. It's guarded by the Superstition Mountains, whose pinnacles seem to break the sky. Volcanic activity from millions of years ago left behind this menacing range. Due to a low grumbling sound, angry crackles, a rumble in the chasms, and lightning strikes atop the crooked spires, the Apache deemed this to be their Thunder God. This deity of the Superstition Mountains protects itself from those intruders seeking only to prosper from its resources.

The Pima urged caution while in the mountains and for centuries have been apprehensive about entering the range. Malevolent happenings occurred behind the fortress of granite, leading to their dire warnings. Their concerns, shared with settlers, are thought to have contributed to its given name. Petroglyphs of bighorn sheep and other patterns reveal the signs of primitive man, and caves discovered in the backcountry were their shelters. It's uncertain how long ago the ancient people realized the formidable powers within the Superstition Mountains, but the Apache roamed the canyons well into the twentieth century.

If it weren't for the last whispers told by one man on his deathbed, the mountains may not have become the subject of widespread mystery. Between intense coughing from a respiratory illness, Jacob Waltz conjured the strength to tell his caretaker, Julia Thomas, about a secret mine filled with gold ore. He was eighty by the time of his death and was known as a simple farmer in Phoenix. His acreage sat against the edge of the Salt River, and usually he kept to himself. He often paid in gold for items he needed, drawing some speculation, but the truth of its source was withheld until the morning of his passing in 1891.

The Lost Dutchman Gold Mine. *Jessica Laughlin.*

Although he was referred to as the "Dutchman," he was an immigrant from Germany. He moved to America and eventually to California during the height of the gold rush. He was scholarly, and it's rumored that he had some education in geology, contributing to his knack in finding ore. Why he chose to come to Arizona Territory from California is unknown, but Waltz was not unfamiliar with prospecting, nor was he ignorant of its dangers. According to legend, he found an entrance to a cave of golden walls somewhere in the Superstition Mountains. It's assumed that he never told a soul and only took what he needed. The evidence is inconclusive, but under his bed there was an opulent matchbox containing veins of gold set in quartz, alongside jewelry and other pieces.

Unsure how to proceed with the information, Thomas was in a predicament after he died. The treasure was in the mountains, but she didn't know where it was hidden. The wilderness was too harsh for her own personal exploration, so she enlisted the help of others. Unlike the Dutchman, she couldn't keep the secret, and this led to the origins of a never-ending search for the gold. Throughout her life, she attempted to unearth the location, but her efforts only intrigued the masses. The forlorn appearance of the mountains added to the mystery. Over the years, numerous people have died in the Superstitions. Some of the casualties were curious prospectors. Many of these reports were further tainted by the unusual circumstances of their deaths. Treasure hunters compelled to discover the mine cast an array of broad theories. It's oftentimes difficult to discern truth from myth, and perhaps it's all become collectively a part of one fable.

After the introduction of the Peralta Stones in the mid-twentieth century, the legend became that much more fascinating. A set of four engraved stone slabs were randomly stumbled upon near Apache Junction, adjacent to the western Superstition Mountains. Various concepts regarding their significance emerged. Each heavy stone, measuring about a foot long, feature rudimentary drawings and Spanish words. A horse, witch, cross, and other shapes carved into the stones are clues thought to lead to the Peralta gold mine.

The Peraltas were a wealthy Spanish family of Sonora, Mexico, with roots dating to their colonization efforts during Spain's occupation of present-day California, Arizona, and New Mexico. Their influence began during the latter 1700s and prevailed for decades. Some researchers think that the Peralta family mined the area. While a shadowy history surrounds their story, some family members, accompanied by a large party, were supposedly on their way back to Mexico with gold in 1848. They were attacked by Apache warriors, and only a few of them escaped. In the chaos, the heavy slabs were discarded to lie in the sand until a century later. If factual, it's a thread linking truth to Jacob Waltz's dying revelation, as he could have come across the Peralta mine.

The presence of these stones has encouraged both imagination and skepticism. Concealed in the desert terrain, lizards and rattlesnakes slithered by these slabs for years before they were seen. Finding them was one thing, but breaking their code is another. Appearing on one of the stones, the witch, wearing a pointed hat, is symbolic of the distinctive peak of Weavers Needle. In this same respect, a concave heart shape on one of the stones fits perfectly together with a complementary heart stone. Underneath, within the heart shape, are the engraved numerals of 1847 and 10. This could have been the year the Peraltas discovered the mine; they were supposedly ambushed on their way back to Mexico in 1848. On the contrary, the numbers could simply be map coordinates or codes identifiable only by the family.

One year after Jacob Waltz died, gold was discovered to the western side of the Superstition Mountains, and the small mining town of Goldfield sprang to life. Because of this, skeptics of the story are convinced that the gold was already found in 1892. The caveat is that the location of Goldfield merely scrapes the outer boundary of the Superstitions, whereas Waltz told Thomas that the gold was within the mountains. The presence of gold at one site doesn't discredit the existence of another—at least this is what the gold seekers believe. The broad community of contemporary prospectors continuously uncover hints in the patterns and maps. Only time will tell how the story ends, but the Lost Dutchman sure gave us all an intriguing puzzle to ponder in the meantime.

Legends of the Grand Canyon

As the first glow of the sun peers over the Grand Canyon in the morning, a natural lightshow begins. Watching from the plateau, the horizon awakens. A veil of darkness is gradually lifted and pulled by the weight of the sun. The shadows against the canyon walls move upward in unison. In the dramatic rise, pure beauty is revealed. Each ledge and quiet corner become illuminated. The colors appear in various shades, mixing in the atmosphere to a golden-honey hue. During this break of dawn, life in the canyon stirs. Birds swiftly begin their sweet chirping. Squirrels scurry along the branches of the juniper and ponderosa pine. Bighorn sheep, in no particular hurry, meander casually along the rocky rim.

The Grand Canyon has been forming for billions of years. The subtle process of erosion, among other factors, forced the canyon to widen and deepen. The Colorado River began carving the canyon into its present appearance about 6 million years ago. Once the progression began, it

The canyon cliffrose. *Jessica Laughlin.*

never stopped. To this day, the canyon is still reshaping and shifting. In the smallest of ways, the flow of water trickling over rocks carries pieces of smaller stones. These fragments cut into the sediment. Over so many years, the friction of nature created this special landscape. Even in the minute crevices, life exists. Each species has its own perspective of their importance within the ecosystem. The smallest of creatures, burrowing into their homes

The Grand Canyon from the South Rim. *Jessica Laughlin.*

on the canyon floor, have no comprehension of the view from the plateau. As we look at the mesmerizing scene, the thought of this natural wonder's enormity is difficult to comprehend. The elements collide here, as does our own existence in connection to something so much larger than ourselves.

John Wesley Powell was the first man to document the enormity of the Grand Canyon. He had previously fought in the Civil War for the Union army, where he was wounded in battle and lost his right forearm. His military service earned him the ranking of major, and this title contributed to his future endeavors. After his service, he went back to his interest in geology. He became a professor in Illinois and was a curator of artifacts for the Illinois Natural History Society Museum. His curiosity in researching living organisms went hand in hand with a longing to explore. At the age of thirty-five, and with funding from the U.S. government, he organized an ambitious surveying expedition of the Colorado River, which commenced in Green River, Wyoming.

The year was 1869, and the party consisted of ten men, some of whom were veterans of the war. Those selected for the mission possessed survival instincts and were skilled hunters. Their basic wooden boats carried them through the Green River tributary until it reached the Colorado River near southeastern Utah. They persisted through bending corridors of slender canyons so tall and narrow that only a ribbon of blue could be seen overhead. This sliver of sky was all that remained of the world they knew before as they entered northern Arizona. Powell conveyed the feeling of the passageway: "We have an unknown distance yet to run, an unknown river to explore. What falls there are, we know not; what rocks beset the channel, we know not; what walls rise over the river, we know not."

Every time they reached a turn, the water could erratically change from a steady stream into a volatile rapid. Clashing against the rocks, they often were thrown from their boats. Three of the explorers chose to leave the journey early, having underestimated the powerful swells inside the Grand Canyon, and their courage had waned. Certain that the rapids ahead would be worse than those they already forged, they parted by foot, taking their chances on finding a settlement, but these men vanished instead. The remainder of his party survived through the canyon, and their voyage ended by the entry of the Virgin River, near St. Thomas, Nevada.

Powell eloquently wrote about the perilous voyage and the impact the Grand Canyon had on him in *The Exploration of the Colorado River and Its Canyons*. Throughout his career, he urged for the protection of land, Native people, and natural resources. By leading with his passions, he gave us a personal glimpse of the canyon's majesty from his own eyes. Having felt the whitewater splashing against his skin, perhaps the spirit of the river entered his body. Through his efforts, he laid the foundation for its protection for years to come. His wise words recognized the fragility found in even the mightiest of landscapes when placed solely in the care of mankind.

This masterpiece traces the story of time itself not only from a geological stance, as Powell so avidly pursued, but also from those who first inhabited the land. From the varied petroglyphs, we gather details about their ancient culture, but in stories living on through their descendants, we gain a better insight. The Grand Canyon is a nexus for several Native tribes and is the sacred location of many creation stories. The Hopi believe that near the confluence of the Colorado and Little Colorado Rivers, their people surfaced from a path to the underworld called the Sipapuni. Similarly, the Zuni also regard their origins to be within the canyon at Ribbon Falls. Both the Hopi and Zuni migrated throughout the Southwest, but their heritage flows back to the canyon depths.

The Hualapai and Havasupai tribes are intertwined and connected to the western region of the canyon. Their reservations are adjacent to the national

Walpi maidens, Hopi. Walpi, Arizona. *Edward S. Curtis, circa 1906, Library of Congress.*

park. Although this side is less visited than the South Rim, the Hualapai reservation has a village and a skywalk attraction. To the east of the Hualapai reservation, the Havasupai live in a remote location. Their village of Supai is eight miles from the nearest road and may be reached by helicopter, mule, or hiking trail. Since the 1930s, the U.S. Postal Service has utilized a mule train to deliver mail to their post office. Often this requires twenty-two mules, and the round trip for the mail carrier is usually eight hours. Though isolated in its location, with advanced planning, visitors make the trip to Supai to swim in the Havasupai Falls. This series of five turquoise waterfalls and crystal-clear pools are set against cliffs of sandstone.

The North Rim of the Grand Canyon is noted for its solitude, although there are lodging and amenities. To the east, however, the Navajo reservation almost entirely borders the national park and offers fewer conveniences. The South Rim is by far the most visited, due to the ease of access and landmarks. In 1901, the Santa Fe Railroad created a route to the Grand Canyon off its main line in Williams. The settlement in the forest became a hub for boarding the steam train. This newly laid track turned traveling to the canyon into a daylong excursion and prompted more development. The Fred Harvey Company was a partner of the Santa Fe Railroad and built hotels, restaurants, and other facilities near the railway to accommodate tourists. They were a dynamic duo, making travel to the Southwest trendy and uncomplicated.

The El Tovar Hotel was the first major hotel to be built in the Grand Canyon and opened its doors in 1905. Constructed on the edge, it was an elegant complement to the views. Not only was it comfortable, but it also possessed a rustic aesthetic throughout the interior. The grand dining room featured exposed beams and a large stone fireplace. Every detail had an interconnection with the surroundings, which made it all the more appealing to tourists seeking authenticity. The interior design of the El Tovar was in large part attributed to the talent of a creative woman named Mary Colter.

Colter had worked for the Fred Harvey Company for a few years as a designer before her assignment at the Grand Canyon. She was gifted in integrating interior spaces with the environment. Although she was in her thirties, her brilliance was groundbreaking, as this new region had yet to establish a style. She found inspiration in the Indigenous cultures and immersed herself in them. Her work never attempted to outweigh the setting. There was certainly a difference in her design approach, and her talents were noticed. She was promoted to lead architect, and her first project under this title would be the Hopi House.

Front entrance of the El Tovar Hotel, circa 1905. *Grand Canyon National Park Museum Collection.*

Group of American Indians singing, the Hopi Building, Grand Canyon, circa 1905. *Library of Congress.*

There was a need for a location dedicated to the sale of Indian crafts near the hotel, and this is why Hopi House was a priority for the company. Colter's vision in modeling the building after a traditional pueblo paid homage to the Indigenous cultures and provided tribes with a space to coexist within the advancing economy of tourism. The Hopi House bridged a divide by respectfully showcasing Native artwork to travelers unfamiliar with the region. She probably had an increased compassion for those who struggled to be heard, as she had likely confronted obstacles as an architect in a traditionally male-dominated profession.

She remained with the Fred Harvey Company throughout her career, completing more than twenty projects throughout the Southwest. Her work in the Grand Canyon alone includes Desert View Watchtower, Lookout Studio, Hermit's Rest, Bright Angel Lodge, and Phantom Ranch. Although she never married, Colter spent her time in devotion to her craft and broke through gender barriers. She never had children but delivered a legacy instead. Women like Colter were unusual in this era, but she redefined the image of what they were capable of achieving. The distinguished architectural style of the region is still influenced by her concepts.

Opposite: East-facing exposure of Lookout Studio, circa 1915. *National Park Service.*

Above: Watchtower at sunrise. *George Grant, 1935, National Park Service.*

Before leisurely travel was commonplace, thrill-seeking individuals were braving the canyon in the late 1800s. The earliest mule rides along the Bright Angel Trail were guided by a cowboy hat–wearing, fortune-seeking prospector named John Hance. He arrived looking for ore and used an ancient Havasupai trail to scale the sidewall to the bottom. In those days, the trail wasn't four feet wide, and it was dangerous. Hance worked the eight-mile trail by hand, smoothing out the rough patches, and then began offering tours to campers. Other men of similar intentions started to appear. They shared a love of the canyon, but they could foresee its value as a tourist destination. In the following years, the original Bright Angel Lodge, built by James Thurber, was made of wooden logs and offered campsites on the property. It would later be redeveloped by the Fred Harvey Company.

Of those who emerged by the turn of the century, the Kolb brothers are honored as the first professional photographers living within the canyon. The medium was rather new, so they were pioneers in both regards. Originally from Pennsylvania, Ellsworth Kolb arrived by train in 1901, and his brother, Emery, joined him the following year. They were both in their twenties and intrepid outdoorsmen who looked at the canyon as a giant playground. Sometimes they would go to extremes to capture the perfect shot, like climbing on swing ladders and straddling the brink. In addition to souvenir booklets of their photos, tourists paid for their portraits to be taken atop mules on the trail. They built a studio cabin next to the Bright Angel trailhead and worked to complete the property for a decade. When Emery married and had a daughter, she was raised against the background of the Grand Canyon. Ellsworth ultimately moved to Los Angeles, but Emery remained behind with his family and camera. He took photographs until he was ninety-six. His passing in 1976 marked the end of a bygone era.

Nowadays, the South Rim retains much of the same appeal it had in the early 1900s because it was designated as a national park in 1919. Federal protection prevented the Grand Canyon from becoming too commercialized. Because it was saved, someone is seeing the grandest view for the first time on a lookout somewhere along that broad rim. Their sight of the splendor is like poetry in visual form, but it's beyond just the view. Even those who are blind can hear the music of nature. They can smell the sweet fragrance of

Photographers suspended on climber's rope in the Grand Canyon. *Kolb Brothers, 1908, Library of Congress.*

Native American seated on the edge of the Grand Canyon, Arizona, circa 1909–32. *Library of Congress.*

the canyon cliffrose, growing on sturdy branches of the shrubs. The spirit of the canyon is felt just as much as it is seen.

Here on the plateau of the canyon country and into its hollowness below, one must abandon the kind of man-made utopias we've all come to know too well—the hum of leaf-blowers tidying up planted lawns and the smell of dewy grass after the sprinkler cycle. This raw land of rock, water, and earth maintains itself without our interference. There are no suburban sidewalks here, but endless miles of paths to which there are no end. The only walls are those nature intended. With all of this in mind, the sun begins to fade into the horizon far out of reach. The shadows reappear as they make their curtain call. The air turns cooler, breezier, as a falcon soars overhead in the closing moments. The canyon will replenish itself by morning—imperceptibly, but slightly changing, as it has for billions of years.

The Apache Kid

In the year 1860, the U.S. government was pushing ahead with its agenda for the Southwest. It was marked pointedly by conflicts between settlers and Native tribes. The Apache in particular had a reputation for confronting their enemies directly with force. In these days, Geronimo was participating in the effort to drive settlers out of the territory and face off against the army. All of this was unfolding when the Apache Kid was born. He was given the name Haskay-bay-nay-natyl, meaning "brave and tall, destined to come to a mysterious end." Like a prophecy, he surely must have thought about his destiny each time he heard his name.

For being among the most infamous outlaws the Southwest encountered, the Apache Kid's history is vague. This isn't all that uncommon, though, because tribal records were not thoroughly documented. Rather than facts, we have partial truths, painting a hazy picture of his childhood. What we do know is that he was born near the Aravaipa Canyon. One theory suggests that he was captured by the Yuma as a boy and lived in servitude prior to being found by the U.S. military, where he became an orphan upon his release. This could explain how he was almost like an adopted son to Al Sieber, who ironically was chief of scouts in leading operations to track Apache rebels.

When the San Carlos Reservation was designated in 1871, scouts like Sieber were tasked in subduing the Apache. Because "Haskay-bay-nay-natyl" was hard to say and remember, he was simply called the "Apache Kid." With the guidance of Sieber, he was groomed to become an Indian scout himself. Indians working for the government against their own tribes had existed for some years beforehand, and Sieber likely found it only logical that his son should become one of them. He was intelligent and advanced through the ranks, which pleased those in authority. While he was doing well in his position as a sergeant, he was at odds with his own Native people and his sense of self.

This strange dynamic brought about a struggle between two opposing identities. There were the traits he shared with other Apache, but his home life with Sieber was among white society. We'll never know his true feelings, but one can guess that he had complex thoughts about his own heritage. To further complicate matters, he may have also reconnected with his biological parents, now confined to the reservation. This is assumed due to an event that started out as an attempt to avenge his biological father's death on the reservation. If this hadn't occurred, it's likely that the Apache Kid would have continued to outshine his peers to the pride of Sieber.

The Apache Kid. *Jessica Laughlin.*

One unfortunate day, Sieber departed San Carlos on a short business trip and entrusted the Apache Kid to supervise. This was obviously a mistake, and whether the kid participated or not, a drunken party happened on his patrol. An alcoholic drink made from corn, tiswin, was passed around. In their delirium and mayhem, the Kid's biological father was killed. The perpetrator fled immediately but was found and shot by the Apache Kid in a flash of revenge. In the company of other Indian scouts, they all made a run for the hills, knowing what their punishment would entail if they stayed.

When Sieber returned, he was obviously filled with disappointment by the Apache Kid's actions and angry at the disorder and murders committed on the reservation in his absence. Urgently, he called for a cavalry to find the scouts, but even with the power of the military, they were difficult to locate. Their behavior was now seen as defiance, and Sieber was becoming impatient. Finding it too challenging to stay on the run, the scouts decided that they would return and suffer the consequences.

When they arrived to meet with the scorned Sieber, he demanded they place their weapons on the ground. Some of them complied, but not all of them were willing to leave their fate to chance. Shots were fired, and in the chaos, Sieber was struck in the ankle by a stray bullet. He couldn't pursue them when injured, so the scouts made a split-second choice to escape again. On the loose for a few weeks, they may have found it harder to survive than expected. Looking over their shoulders, they laid low against the encroaching detainment.

The Apache Kid found a way to deliver a message to General Miles. The Kid swore that they would return to the reservation if the cavalry would cease their pursuit. In late June 1887, they arrived at San Carlos, prepared to receive the penalties for their crimes. After a brief deliberation, they were sentenced to death by firing squad. This verdict seemed too severe to the general. He very well could have had a soft spot for the once law-abiding kid who had shown initial promise. Due to his reasoning, the scouts weren't executed and instead were sentenced to ten years in Alcatraz.

Condemning them to the feared prison in the San Francisco Bay sent a strong message. Unable to walk and using crutches, Sieber showed no compassion for the outcome. The scouts were sent off to Alcatraz, and for all they knew, they would be there for the foreseeable future. Like the dense fog rolling over the frigid water, details of their life behind bars are mostly lost to history. One can only speculate how miserable they were, as prisoners as well as Apache in a time where they were often treated inhumanely. In a surprise turn of events, their case came under scrutiny due to the fact that they were tried under court-martial, but technically the Indian scouts were not in the military. It was determined that they should be released, pending a retrial subject to the verdict of a civil case.

When they arrived again in Arizona Territory, they were brought to the Globe jailhouse and held for various charges. The Apache Kid and three of his accomplices were sentenced to seven years in the Yuma Territorial Prison for the crime of attempted murder. Having spent more than a year in Alcatraz, they dreaded another seven in Yuma. After the verdict was given in October 1889, they were soon en route to their final destination. A stagecoach was arranged to escort the prisoners to Casa Grande, where they would board a train for Yuma.

All was going to plan. They camped overnight halfway and the next morning were back on the trail. Then they reached a hard-to-pass section. An abrupt incline presented a problem, for the horses couldn't pull the weight of all the men. The guards had no choice but to allow the prisoners to walk, which meant releasing their bound feet. The Apache Kid rode with the driver, who had already made it beyond the hill when gunfire was heard. The prisoners ambushed the sheriff and deputy by overtaking them in a surprise attack. Evidently, they shot the sheriff, but the deputy died of a heart attack. After they gathered the guns, they went over the hill to the stagecoach, where they shot the driver and freed the Apache Kid. Other than the Apache, the only other prisoner being transported to Yuma that day was a Mexican man who had been convicted for stealing horses. This man was also shot but survived alongside the driver.

Taking the horses, the Apache got away and disappeared into the unknown. They were never seen again. The two surviving men made it to town, and when the news returned to Sieber, he sent another army to find the renegades. They were long gone though. The snowstorms made it difficult to trace their path. For years, people claimed to see the Apache Kid, whose face was on every wanted poster across the region. They blamed him for terrible crimes, even without evidence. Instead of being seen as a person, he became a rebellious Indian figure on the cover of dime novels.

There's no telling where his path ended; perhaps he did go forth to live a life of crime, but this is unsubstantiated. Rumors drove wild speculations. One week he was reported to be dead, whereas the next he was seen alive. The most common narrative, though unverified, states that he was murdered by a posse in eastern New Mexico's Cibola National Forest in 1894. The remote site of his apparent death is defined by a marker, near Apache Kid Peak, but his body was never located. The prophecy was true all along: the tall and brave man's destiny became a mystery.

TOMBSTONE AND THE GUNFIGHT AT THE O.K. CORRAL

In the Sonoran Desert of southern Arizona, Tombstone was a thriving town in the late nineteenth century. Prior to Ed Schieffelin discovering silver in 1877, the prospector was warned by a soldier that the only stone he would find in the area would be that of his own "tombstone." Steadfast in his goal, when he struck silver, he fittingly named his mine Tombstone. The town followed suit and was established in 1879. Soon, it was swarming with eager people.

Virgil Earp was one of these men who came riding into town with his intentions set on prospecting. He was living in Prescott and working as a deputy U.S. marshal, but when he landed in Tombstone, he was also granted the role of city marshal. His brother Wyatt, who was then a lawman in Dodge City, Kansas, thought that it would be beneficial to join him. Everyone was

The Earp brothers and Doc. *Jessica Laughlin.*

talking about the town with the crazy name, and evidently, Wyatt liked to be in on the action. With his wife, Mattie, they departed Kansas and headed for Tombstone. The youngest of the Earps, Morgan, was also compelled to reunite with them. They purchased adjoining lots, essentially connecting their homes to create a kind of small compound. Along with their wives, they settled into the frontier town and set out to make a name for themselves.

Around this time, Wyatt's friend Doc Holliday entered with a gal named Kate by his side. It could be that Wyatt convinced Doc to move to Tombstone, but on the frontier, everyone relocated often. As a backstory to their friendship, Doc and Wyatt had originally met in Texas and likely became acquainted at a poker table. Their paths crossed again in Dodge City, where Doc was credited in coming to Wyatt's aid when he was outnumbered by a group of cowboys. Their friendship seemed to intersect at different points in their lives.

Although Doc had once been a dentist in Georgia, he struggled with severe tuberculosis, and the dry climate helped his lungs. He also knew that he would likely die of the disease, giving him a darker outlook on life that took the form of excessive drinking, gambling, and saying what he pleased.

Left: Wyatt Earp. *Author's collection.*

Right: Doc Holliday. *Noah H. Rose, circa 1880s, Denver Public Library Special Collections.*

Although Wyatt was a man of the law, his friendship with Doc became as close as that with his own brothers. He found Doc's antics amusing, and he was sharp when it came to poker. Wyatt respected these qualities about Doc because even though he wore the badge, he also gravitated toward the wilder side of life. There was plenty of this to go around in Tombstone, and as the town grew, so did the casinos, saloons, and brothels.

Virgil appointed Wyatt and Morgan to serve as deputies. As these handsome men in uniform walked down Allen Street, they were surely getting their share of smiles from the ladies. By this time, Tombstone was bursting with casinos like the Crystal Palace and Oriental Saloon. The good and moral citizens lived under the overarching population of gamblers, bandits, prostitutes, crooks, and profiteers. There was an endless array of crime to police, and it kept the brothers fairly busy. They weren't by any means prudes, though, and they were known to like the nightlife just as much as Doc.

Wyatt's wife, Mattie, was often at home while he was either out policing or gambling. He soon became enamored of another gorgeous woman named Josephine Sarah Marcus. It's widely believed that "Josie" could have been an entertainer or working girl. A photo identified as Josie,

The Crystal Palace Saloon, Tombstone, Arizona, circa 1880s. *Author's collection.*

wearing a sheer black robe over her voluptuous body, surfaced later, further validating this theory. They were both entangled with other people for some time after first laying eyes on each other. While they were not married immediately, they were obviously having an affair before he divorced Mattie. Josie was also the lover of Johnny Behan, the county sheriff.

Considering their authority in Tombstone, the Earps were loved by some and disliked by others. Their presence particularly irritated the McLaury and Clanton brothers, a band of cowboys who were thought to be murderous thieves. During the late 1800s in the territory, the term *cowboy* wasn't used to describe moral ranch hands. It was instead applied to cattle rustlers. The gang not only sold beef to restaurants but also had other criminal enterprises. The Earps were well aware of the cowboys' aversion to the law, and word began to surface that they were their targets.

Ike Clanton, who was the ringleader of the gang, spewed his grievances about them wherever he found a willing audience. Simply put, they were on his turf, and he couldn't move about freely under their watch. The cowboys' antics grew even more taunting and aggressive. Before long, they were threatening the Earps' lives. The brothers now either had to confront their

Left: "Kaloma," considered to be Josephine Earp. *Author's collection.*

Right: Josephine Earp. *Author's collection.*

enemies or be run out of Tombstone. With the help of their loyal friend Doc, they chose to stand their ground in the only way those in the Wild West could understand.

On the afternoon of October 26, 1881, both sides met outside the O.K. Corral. Although the gunfight lasted a mere thirty seconds, three of the cowboys were killed: Frank and Tom McLaury and Billy Clanton. The other two in the gang, Ike Clanton and Billy Claiborne, somehow got away unscathed. Virgil and Morgan received bullet wounds, but with medical attention, they survived. The chaos caused Tombstone to be divided. Some stood on the side of law and order, and others thought that it was an overreach of the Earps' authority.

In the following days, Ike Clanton gathered public sympathy, especially when the executed bodies were paraded down Allen Street in black coffins before being laid to rest at the Boothill Cemetery. After all the commotion, the Earps and Doc were put on trial at the Tombstone Courthouse. Sheriff Behan already had his issues with Wyatt and Josie, so he was vehemently in support of their guilt. The sensational trial gained national attention, but ultimately none of them was found guilty. Doc, in all his swagger, walked out of the courtroom a free man alongside the Earps. This further enraged Ike Clanton.

The long-running feud was far from over. The remaining cowboys retaliated by shooting Virgil and causing permanent damage to his arm. They also killed Morgan by firing through a glass window at a pool hall, and the bullet hit his spine. The loss of his brother drove Wyatt to a point where the law no longer mattered, and he sought only vengeance in what has been coined the "Vendetta Ride." During this period, he took revenge against the men who he deemed had taken part in the assassination of Morgan. Doc rode with Wyatt for as long as he could, helping him seek his own form of justice, all the while knowing he was dying.

In the end, they all gave up on Tombstone. The Earps moved to California and then from there to other boomtowns in Nevada. Ironically, the two women in Wyatt's life seemed to switch roles: It's alleged that Mattie became a prostitute. Josie and Wyatt were married and were together for the rest of their lives, both living into their eighties. As for Doc, he headed to Glenwood Springs, Colorado, to receive treatment in a sanitarium, where he died in 1887 at the age of thirty-six.

The O.K. Corral in present-day Tombstone, Arizona. *Jessica Laughlin, 2024.*

Top: The Bird Cage Theatre. *Lee Russell, circa 1940, Library of Congress.*

Bottom: A night of poker at the Bird Cage Theatre. *Jessica Laughlin.*

By 1893, the mines had run dry in Tombstone, and its residents were generally gone or buried in the cemetery. The town could have been abandoned, but it survived to tell their story. Tombstone became connected to the righteous fight of good versus evil in western lore. The Earps and Doc were vigilante heroes, with their story becoming the inspiration for countless films, including the iconic 1993 film *Tombstone*. Over time, the site became a popular travel destination, with reenactments of the Gunfight at the O.K. Corral. The Crystal Palace Saloon continues to serve drinks and meals by waitresses dressed in costumed attire. In the finished basement of the Bird Cage Theatre, where the longest poker game in history was played around the clock, the table remains empty. Instead of those whistling crowds, mannequins sit in the balcony seats as if they are waiting for the show to begin.

Tombstone has become a time capsule, and maybe it stands against the march of time because of an inherent feeling within all of us that wants to return to the days of real connection, where entertainment wasn't found on screens but in life itself. There was a freedom to people's existence then. Although their lives were oftentimes short and in a constant state of lust and desire, they weren't just living—they were really *alive*.

PART III

SOUTHERN NEVADA

Jim Butler and the Queen of the Silver Camps

Jim Butler came from a family of miners who settled in California's El Dorado County during the gold rush. Although he was just a boy, he was immersed in the bustling setting of mining camps, where striking it rich, or losing it all trying, was the nature of life. While his father's dreams of ore ran through his veins, he never anticipated that his own future would be in mining. Rather, after witnessing the hard life of his parents, he chose the opposite. He moved to Nevada with his wife, Belle, and operated a hay farm in the remote desert, north of present-day Tonopah. Rural life wasn't easy, but the couple lived comfortably.

Jim Butler. *Jessica Laughlin.*

In middle age, Butler settled into a farmer's life, but he went prospecting as a pastime. On his way to visit friends, he stopped for the evening with his mule at Tonopah Springs. Settling in for the night, the mule wandered off. He grabbed a rock to throw in its direction, but the rock felt heavier than most. He would later find that it was loaded with silver. Had his stubborn mule not strayed, the great silver and gold booms in Nevada during the twentieth century may not have happened.

Butler became a wealthy man, and the town of Tonopah rose to acclaim in the early 1900s. Merchants and hardworking miners arrived for their share of the wealth in the "Queen of the Silver Camps." Those who came initially possessed a tolerance for a gritty lifestyle. In order to capitalize on the rush of a boomtown, one endured many inconveniences. Running water wasn't available, the weather could be extreme, and common amenities were hard to find. The silver lining of living in such conditions was the money to be made, and wealthy individuals invested in the mining enterprises.

Remote boomtowns like Tonopah wrote their own rules and were far from refined living. Working conditions were hard, and hundreds died working in the confines of dark mines. At the old Tonopah cemetery, now oddly located next to the infamous Clown Motel, simple wooden headstones mark the end of the trail for those who came for the dream of riches only to meet

View of Tonopah, Nevada. *F.W. Sheelor, circa 1913, Library of Congress.*

a brutal fate. One of the most recognized ghost stories to come from this period was that of Rose, a lady of the night who was murdered at the hands of a familiar lover in room 502 of the Mizpah Hotel. While this haunting moment lingers on the fifth floor, her immortal spirit is said to have never left the premises. Hundreds of Mizpah guests attest to their experiences with the Lady in Red. As it was a distinguished hotel during its prime, thousands passed through its brass doors. The Mizpah remains open for reservations and serves as a historical centerpiece in downtown Tonopah. Because of its secrets and violent past, paranormal activity at the hotel is elevated, and the Mizpah consistently ranks as one of the most haunted hotels in America.

Jim Butler and his mule in Tonopah, Nevada. *Author's collection.*

Death Valley Scotty

In Death Valley, the heat from the blazing summer sun is relentless, reaching uninhabitable temperatures as high as a recorded 134 degrees. Vast valleys of mountains and dunes seem bereft of life. Emptiness, stillness, and heat warn one not to venture too far into this abyss. Going off the beaten track here could be lethal, and some have met this terrible fate.

The legend of Death Valley is not only found in its raw setting but also in the curiosity of what drove those crazed enough to brave its elements before it became a national park. For decades prior to the paved roads, air-conditioned visitors' center, and scenic byways, this unforgiving land belonged only to those restless enough to pierce its mystery in search of wealth. It was the frontier of madmen, and the maddest of them all was Death Valley Scotty.

Far from Death Valley, in the small Kentucky town of Cynthiana, Walter Scott was born on a cool September day in 1872. His bright blue eyes gazed at his mother, and the innocence of her youngest child filled her soul with purpose as she cradled him close to her heart. If only she could have lived to see his future, but she died shortly thereafter. The now motherless child was raised on the family horse farm, where he spent much of his younger years developing his riding skills. As his talents matured, so did his wandering spirit. At eleven years old, he ran away to join two of his older brothers in Wells, Nevada, where they worked at a horse ranch.

Leaving home as an adolescent had an effect on his personality, as he realized he could charm strangers along the way. With only himself to rely on, he became obsessed with obtaining a fortune of his own. Once out west, he began a lifelong pursuit of opportunity. While his brothers could only do so much for him as a kid, he landed his first job doing tasks for a survey company, which led him on assignment to the edge of Death Valley along the southern Nevada and California border. Wise beyond his years, Scotty saw promise in a land that most feared; there was money to be had in its cultivation, even if he didn't have the means to do it himself. This ever-present void filled him with a desire to succeed no matter the consequences.

When he was sixteen, an opportunity came along to join Buffalo Bill's Wild West Show. As a talented rider, he spent the next decade traveling and performing stunts on horseback. This gave him a taste of fame. In 1900,

Scotty's Castle. *Jessica Laughlin.*

he met his future wife, Ella, in New York City. After they married, he left the show and moved to Colorado, where he ventured into mining, but this was unsuccessful. It was during this time that Scotty began lying to wealthy businessmen about mines he owned in Death Valley. The more he convinced trusting souls to invest in his company, the more elaborate the hoax became. He eventually abandoned his wife and child in an attempt to find a legitimate gold site to support his false claims.

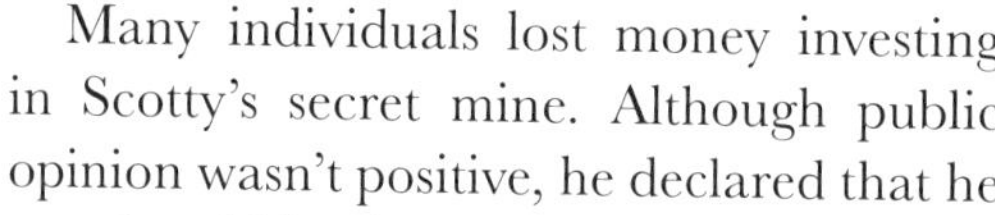

Many individuals lost money investing in Scotty's secret mine. Although public opinion wasn't positive, he declared that he struck gold in the desert. Most investors came to understand that Scotty was a con man. However, Albert Johnson refused to accept the truth. Johnson lost his father in a train collision when he was a younger man, and the accident left him suffering from a spinal injury. His longing to ride like the cowboys of the West and to live a life beyond the aristocracy of his family's fortune were perhaps factors in his continuing friendship with Scotty.

Albert's wife, Bessie, found herself increasingly alone in Chicago as he spent more time in the West. He grew to appreciate the desert, and the heat helped his ailments. Most of all, he enjoyed Scotty's company and his recollections of wild adventures. The more time he spent in Scotty's world, the more he imagined living the western lifestyle himself. He decided to build a vacation home in Death Valley, which was in California but just over the line from Nevada. One can imagine the reluctance Bessie may have felt about this strange idea, but she eventually agreed to his plans.

Building such a property in the faraway desert was an incredible feat that involved years of construction. In current times, it would be outrageously expensive and problematic, much less doing so in the 1920s. However, with the encouragement of Scotty, the Johnsons embarked on the project of their lives. When the mansion was complete, it was similar to a Spanish castle. In the middle of nowhere, the complex contained various buildings, twenty-five bedrooms, decorative fountains, and carved wooden ceilings. The castle was also self-sustaining, as the water pumped from a spring was also used to generate electricity.

Opposite: Death Valley Scotty. *Jessica Laughlin.*

Above: Albert Johnson and Death Valley Scotty, circa 1930. *National Park Service.*

Scotty's Castle, aerial view, looking northwest, Death Valley. *Jack E. Boucher, Library of Congress.*

Scotty was given a guest house, and he also had a room within the mansion. He became a rather permanent house guest, entertaining the Johnsons and their visitors with his stories. Their affluent friends were likely enthralled by his amusing tales, and he became an icon even during his own lifetime. One could suggest that he conned his way into the couple's lives, but on the other hand, he was thought to be the best friend Albert ever had.

Bessie was killed in an automobile accident in 1943 while driving on the treacherous Towne Pass in Death Valley. After her passing, Albert was distraught and spent less time at the property. He eventually died five years later of cancer in 1948. Because they didn't have children, they had previously arranged for the castle to be given to their church. However, their final will made it clear that Scotty could reside there indefinitely. Along with all of his secrets, he was laid to rest in 1954 on a hill overlooking the valley he loved. Although he never discovered gold, he became the man behind the castle of Death Valley and one of the most legendary prospectors of all time.

Pioche: The Most Violent of All Mining Towns

Nevada received its statehood in 1864, and this same year, a massive silver vein was discovered in an arid desert region around what would become Pioche. This was in the wake of the 1859 Comstock Lode, the largest and purest deposit of silver ever found in American history. Virginia City, to the eastern side of the Sierras, became a sensation overnight. Subsequently, when the word spread of another silver boom, everyone knew that it was crucial to arrive to the party early. Those who had made no delay in heading to Virginia City to work the mines, open businesses, and buy land reaped the benefits. Therefore, speculators were ready for the bonanza this time in southeastern Nevada.

François Pioche, a wealthy individual from San Francisco, bought out the lone prospector claims that had been surfacing since 1864. By 1870, the population was close to ten thousand. There were more than one hundred saloons and bordellos combined. Unlike Virginia City, which was now sitting next to the state capital in Carson City, the location of Pioche bred a certain kind of detachment from civilization. This made it the ideal hangout for criminals. It's been claimed that seventy-two men were murdered here before the first death by a natural cause. This reveals a lot about the character of the place, as in those days, life itself could kill as easily as a bullet.

These outlaw types drunkenly walked the streets and would pull out their six-shooters at a sideways glace. Within this anarchy, justice was served by the law of the gun. There were so many murders that the Boothill Cemetery was set aside for all the souls who were "buried with their boots on." Simple headstones of wood were inscribed with epitaphs regarding their demise and usually named their killer too.

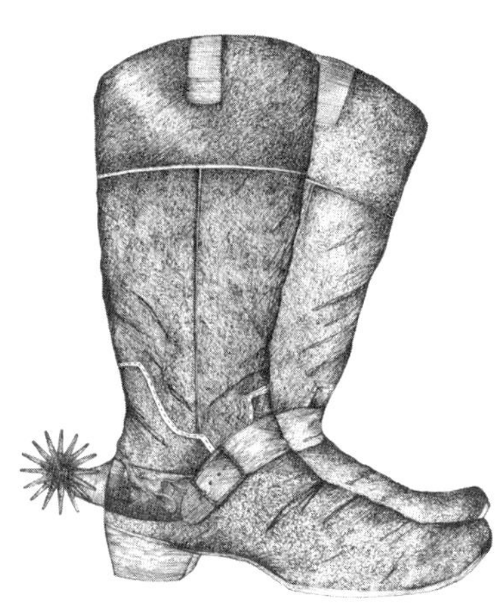

Outlaw boots. *Jessica Laughlin.*

There are other Boothill Cemeteries throughout the West and Southwest, including those famously in Tombstone and Dodge City, but the one in Pioche may just be the most spine-chilling. There are at least one hundred murderers buried among the dead in this dirt cemetery. The

The Lincoln County Courthouse, Pioche, Nevada. *Library of Congress.*

site is deathly silent, other than an old mining bucket rattling in the wind, hanging on a highline wire above. Hats and bottles decorate their solemn graves. A strange feeling hovers when walking the long and languid row as a stranger, reading their names. Andrew Whitlock, killed by Jas Maxwell; Harry Gorman, killed by George Hirsh; and so forth. All their names are etched into these splintered pieces of obscure history.

Pioche wasn't a wholesome city, and its reputation was off to a bad start by the time the plans for a courthouse and jail were underway in 1871. The budget was $26,400, but $25,000 of this amount was funded by the sale of bonds. The construction cost was grossly underestimated, and a year later the debt had risen to $88,000. Pioche finally had a place for its criminals, but it couldn't repay its debts. Over the years, the interest compiled. When it was finally paid in 1937, the cost of the courthouse was almost $1 million. By this time, it was condemned and needed repairs. A century after the whole debacle began, the "Million Dollar Courthouse" reopened in the 1970s as a museum.

Although Pioche is the county seat of the sparsely populated Lincoln County, it's a living ghost town today. Sometimes, however, it's out-of-the way places like Pioche that give us a real perspective of mining camps before their heyday came and went. It's also where you may just hear the sound of those heavy boots walking beside you.

Dusty Dreams of Ore in Goldfield and Rhyolite

Nevada arrived late to the Union, but we wouldn't expect anything less from Lady Luck. Her entrance was bold, with Nevada gaining statehood during the height of the Comstock Lode. It was a wild one from the start, welcoming dreamers and hustlers into its embrace. Its bare desert wasn't for the easily intimidated. It required guts of steel to cross these miles, and those who did became rougher around the edges than they were before.

After enormous lodes of silver were found in Virginia City, Pioche, and Tonopah, a big vein of gold was finally struck in Nevada. Behind the discovery in Goldfield was again Jim Butler of Tonopah, who was now financially able to fund other prospectors in his search for more gold or silver. Two of the men he hired, Harry Stimler and William Marsh, were searching south of Tonopah on a winter's day in December 1902 when strong winds began to move across the valley. This made visibility difficult, but after taking cover during the sandstorm, they happened to spot a glimmer of gold.

Shortly thereafter, the mining districts were built, and in October 1903, the townsite was organized. News spread throughout the country about the next big boomtown. The silver mines had practically dried up in Virginia City, Pioche had passed its glory, and Tonopah was in its prime. Now Goldfield

STAGE

Opposite, top: Stagecoach crossing the desert to Goldfield, Nevada, 1906. *Library of Congress.*

Opposite, bottom: Interior view of the Mohawk Mine, Goldfield, Nevada. *Charles C. Pierce, circa 1905, USC Libraries and California Historical Society.*

Above: Burro-drawn wagon hauling supplies into Goldfield, Nevada, circa 1904. *USC Libraries and California Historical Society.*

would trump them all. People came fast and with momentum. Rich or poor, they had one thing in common: hope. They crossed the deserts on their horses, mules, and stagecoaches. The scruffy miners put up their ramshackle canvas tents, shopkeepers claimed their lots, and the ladies of the night were soon on the scene. Riches could be realized by anyone.

At a rapid pace, Goldfield became a small city in the desert. There were not only casinos and saloons galore but also every amenity or service a person could need to live comfortably. It was not like the hardened camps of the past—it was a modernized, golden city of prosperity. By 1906, the town had electricity, running water, telephone lines, and a railroad depot. There were all sorts of shops and restaurants on Main Street, which had paved sidewalks, remarkably. Over the next two years, Goldfield would secure a courthouse, fire department, and hospital.

Goldfield, Nevada, 1905. *Jessica Laughlin.*

The streets of Goldfield were dynamic, and the town hosted many events. The famed Gans–Nelson boxing match occurred on Labor Day 1906 and drew a crowd of eight thousand spectators. It was considered the "Fight of the Century" and even filmed. There was so much activity in this area that it seemed like the fun would never end.

Even Virgil and Wyatt Earp made an appearance in Goldfield, as the Earps seemed to show up when a place was bound to make history. Virgil became a deputy sheriff of Esmeralda County in January 1905, but his health declined when he came down with pneumonia. He had survived the chaos in Tombstone but succumbed to the complications of his illness in October at the local hospital.

By the spring of 1907, this mining district had become the largest city in Nevada. There were more than twenty thousand people living in Goldfield alone, and thousands more were in Tonopah, twenty-seven miles to the north. This happened to be the same year the prominent Goldfield Hotel began construction. The extravagant building was four stories. Through the entryway, visitors could socialize in the opulent lobby. The architectural details were sophisticated, featuring mahogany walls, ornate pillars, and crystal lighting powered by electricity. Guests could take an elevator to their rooms. The accommodations were stately, with plush bedding, clawfoot bathtubs, running water, and steam heat.

Meanwhile, only seventy-two miles to the south in Rhyolite, near the eastern threshold of Death Valley, there was another gold boom underway. Much like with the birth of Goldfield, two prospectors, Shorty Harris and E.L. Cross, stumbled on quartz covering a hill. It just so happened to be laced with gold. In the following months, if one looked at a panorama of Rhyolite, they would see the sight of countless canvas tents covering the landscape. Just like in Goldfield, the settlement soon had a bank, a stock exchange, social halls, and more. One of the most interesting new businesses was an ice cream parlor, which must have done very well in the hot climate.

While there was much progress by the wealthy individuals with access to capital, there were also folks who had difficulty in sourcing materials to build homes. For miners and their families, they oftentimes added wood siding

Drilling contest on Labor Day, Goldfield, Nevada. *Allen Photo Company, circa 1906, Library of Congress.*

Busy Main Street in Goldfield, Nevada, circa 1905. *USC Libraries and California Historical Society.*

ORSES

around the canvas of their tents. There were also many homes made of bottles. One of the best examples of this originality is in Rhyolite, where a miner named Tom Kelly used fifty thousand bottles he found discarded at local saloons to build a house. While all the other structures in Rhyolite are like ruins, his bottle house has stood the test of time.

In retrospect, Goldfield and Rhyolite would be two of the last boomtowns of their kind. Born in the twentieth century, they existed in between the Old West and a more industrialized America that now stretched from the Atlantic to the Pacific. Automobiles were replacing horses and stagecoaches. Most of the open range was now either government land or privately owned. The coming of the future was upon them all.

Rhyolite's bust came first; in a handful of years, it went from a place of promise to completely hopeless. In 1911, the Montgomery Shoshone mine shut down, and everyone moved. There wasn't a need for electricity anymore, and in 1916, the lights were turned off for good. Goldfield was starting to feel a strain as well, but it hadn't entirely given up. The mines were producing less and less. The spirited town wasn't flourishing anymore. The ominous example of Rhyolite made their worries worse. The population in Goldfield had decreased significantly by 1910, with fewer than two thousand residents, and it only went down from there. This was accelerated by several destructive fires.

Opposite: The Goldfield Hotel, present day. *Jessica Laughlin, 2024.*

This page, top: Abandoned house in Goldfield, Nevada. *Jessica Laughlin, 2024.*

This page, bottom: Abandoned train depot entrances to nowhere in Goldfield, Nevada. *Jessica Laughlin, 2024.*

Ruins of the Cook Bank building, Rhyolite, Nevada. *Jessica Laughlin, 2021.*

Certain prominent structures in Goldfield survived the catastrophic fire of 1923, which tore through downtown and claimed much of its history in the blaze. The Goldfield Hotel was protected, though, and remained open until the 1940s. Since then, the striking hotel has been abandoned. The guests are gone, the rooms are dark, and it looms over the sleepy Main Street. The population today is in the low hundreds, but the Esmeralda County Courthouse is used by the local government. Walking through the silent blocks, preserved historic landmarks sit next to those that are completely dilapidated. Canvas tent fabric hangs off the brittle wood. A rocking chair on a crumbling porch sways with the gentlest breeze. Rhyolite is even lonelier, without a population at all. In the hour before darkness, surrounded by the muted light of these ghost towns, the desert whispers its promises of reclamation.

The frontier wasn't settled by men sitting in fancy faraway offices, writing laws and drawing boundary lines. Rather, it was built by those who knew the dirt under their feet. It was the Native people, the settlers, the wanderers, the drifters, the outlaws, and the saints. Although the gold dust evaporated into the air, we still see a sparkle on the ground now and then. All of their stories

Photograph of a sculpture by Charles A. Szukalski titled *The Last Supper*, Rhyolite, Nevada. *Jessica Laughlin, 2021.*

seem to float together, rising and falling over the mountains and deserts, forever chasing the horizon. They are part of the land, of the rivers and forests between the distances. On the trails of time, they became the legends of the old Southwest.

BIBLIOGRAPHY

Arizona State Parks. "Audrey Headframe." www.azstateparks.com.

———. "Legend of the Lost Dutchman." www.azstateparks.com.

Barrett, S.M. *Geronimo, My Life*. Dover Publications, 2005.

Britannica. "Cultural Life: Phoenix." www.britannica.com.

Carlisle Indian Industrial School Digital Resource Center. "Chapo Geronimo." www.carlisleindian.dickinson.edu/index.php.

City of Phoenix. "City of Phoenix History." www.phoenix.gov.

Cowan, James P. "The Results of Hum Studies in the United States." *9th International Congress on Noise as a Public Health Problem* (2008).

Curtis, Edward S. *The North American Indian: The Complete Portfolios*. Reproduction. Taschen, 2018.

El Palacio—Art, History & Culture of the Southwest. "The Mystery of the Penitentes." December 2019. www.elpalacio.org.

Eppinga, Jane. *Tombstone*. Images of America series. Arcadia Publishing, 2003.

Find a Grave. "Green Berry Ketchum Sr." www.findagrave.com.

———. "James Larkin 'Jim' White." www.findagrave.com.

———. "James L. Butler." www.findagrave.com.

Frémont, John C. *Memoirs of My Life*. Belford, Clark & Company, 1886.

The Gila River Indian Community. "About the Tribe." www.gilariver.org.

The Goldfield Historical Society. "The History of Goldfield." www.goldfieldhistoricalsociety.com.

Gordon, Mark J. "Awakening in Taos: The Mabel Dodge Luhan Story." PBS, 2015.

Grant, Rich. "On the Trail of Kit Carson in Taos." HuffPost, July 21, 2016. www.huffpost.com.

Haralson, Danny. "Did You Know: Pioneer Extraordinaire—The Jack W. Swilling Connection to Arizona and the Gila Valley." *Eastern Arizona Courier*, November, 27, 2016. www.eacourier.com.

Herald Democrat. "Severed Man's Head." April 27, 1901. Via Colorado Historic Newspapers Collection.

Historical Marker Database. "Jerome's Famous Sliding Jail." www.hmdb.org.

———. "Pioche's Boot Hill." www.hmdb.org.

History. "Religious Founder Joseph Smith Killed by Mob." February 9, 2010. history.com.

———. "This Day in History, 1844: Religious Founder Joseph Smith Killed by Mob." February 9, 2010. www.history.com.

Kollenborn, Tom. "Apache Junction: A Short Story." Apache Junction Public Library. www.ajpl.org.

———. "Julia Thomas." Apache Junction Public Library. www.ajpl.org.

LeJeune, Christian. "Blue Hole Cienega Nature Preserve, Santa Rosa, New Mexico Groundwater Monitoring Project Final Report, 2016–2017." Wetwater Environmental Services. www.emnrd.nm.gov.

Milford, Homer. "History of the Los Cerrillos Mining District." Amigos de Cerrillos Hills State Park. www.cerrilloshills.org.

Mullins, Joe H., and James P. Kelly. "The Mystery of the Taos Hum." *Acoustical Society of America* 5, no.4 (1995).

National Geographic Guide to the National Parks of the United States. 6th ed. National Geographic Society, 2009.

National Park Service. "Albert Mussey Johnson." https://www.nps.gov.

———. "Carlisle Federal Indian Boarding School." www.nps.gov.

———. "Carlsbad Caverns National Park, Cave Exploration Milestones." www.nps.gov.

———. "Casa Grande Ruins." www.nps.gov.

———. "El Santuario de Chimayo." www.nps.gov.

———. "Grand Canyon National Park, Arizona." www.nps.gov.

———. "Guadalupe Mountains National Park, Texas." www.nps.gov.

———. "Interesting Facts About Carlsbad Caverns." www.nps.gov.

———. "John Hance." www.nps.gov.

———. "Kolb Studio." www.nps.gov.

———. "Mary Colter and Her Buildings at Grand Canyon." www.nps.gov.

———. "Rhyolite Ghost Town." www.nps.gov.

———. "Scotty's Castle." www.nps.gov.

New Mexico Bureau of Geology and Natural Resources. "Geology of the Taos Area: Geologic Setting." www.geoinfo.nmt.edu.

New Mexico History Museum. "The Gambling Queen of Santa Fe." www.media.newmexicoculture.org.

New Mexico Museum of Art. "History: El Camino Real de Tierra Adentro." www.nmartmuseum.org.

New Mexico Museum of National History & Science. "Taos Plateau Volcanic Field." www.nmnaturalhistory.org.

O.K. Corral. "A Brief History of the Famous Gunfight at the O.K. Corral." www.ok-corral.com.

Paher, Stanley W. *Nevada Ghost Towns & Desert Atlas*. 11th ed. Nevada Publications, 2022.

PBS American Experience. "The Life and Legend of Billy the Kid." www.pbs.org.

———. "The Pardoning of Billy the Kid." www.pbs.org.

PBS Weekend Explorer. "Experience Jim White's Thrill of Discovering the Cave, in His Own Words." www.pbs.org.

Powell, J.W. *The Exploration of the Colorado River and Its Canyons*. Dover Publications, 2012.

Rea, Tom. "Crossing Wyoming: Kit Carson and a Changing West." Online Encyclopedia of Wyoming History, November 26, 2025. www.wyohistory.org.

Riggs, Sarana. "Zuni Ties to the Grand Canyon." Grand Canyon Trust, June 9, 2022. www.grandcanyontrust.org.

Romancito, Rick. "The 1847 Taos Revolt and the History We Must Never Forget." *Taos News*, January 24, 2023. www.taosnews.com.

San Carlos Apache Tribe. "Our History." www.scat-nsn.gov.

Santa Rosa Blue Hole. "About the Blue Hole Santa Rosa New Mexico." www.santarosabluehole.com

Serena, Katie. "Brushy Bill Roberts: The Man Who Claimed to Be Billy the Kid." All That's Interesting, December 25, 2018. www.allthatsinteresting.com.

Silbernagel, Bob. "Disaster Struck When 'The Pathfinder' Got Lost in Colorado." *Daily Sentinel* (Grand Junction, CO), May 28, 2025. www.gjsentinel.com.

St. Louis Art Museum. "1904 St. Louis World's Fair." www.slam.org.

Stratton, Royal B., Lorenzo D. Oatman and Olive A. Oatman. *The Captivity of the Oatman Girls Among the Apache and Mohave Indians*. Dover Publications, 1994.

Taos Pueblo. "About Taos Pueblo." www.taospueblo.com.

Texas State Historical Association. "Black Jack Ketchum Is Captured in New Mexico." www.tshaonline.org.

Tonopah, Nevada. "Tonopah's History." www.tonopahnevada.com.

Turner, Jim. "What History Writes About the Apache Kid." *Globe Miami Times*, May 4, 2010. www.globemiamitimes.com.

UNESCO World Heritage Convention. "Taos Pueblo." www.whc.unesco.org.

U.S. Postal Service. "Mule Train Delivery." www.facts.usps.com.

Verde Valley Archaeology Center and Museum. "Early Inhabitants." www.verdevalleyarchaeology.org.

Visit Taos, New Mexico. "Taos Society of Artists." www.taos.org.

Zier, Christian J. "Kit Carson." History Colorado. https://coloradoencyclopedia.org.

ABOUT THE AUTHOR

Jessica Laughlin combines art, history, and travel in her creative work. Along with *Legends & Lore of the Old Southwest*, she is also the author and illustrator of *The 50 States Bucket List: The Ultimate Journal for a Journey Across America*. She graduated from the Las Vegas Academy of the Arts and received a bachelor's degree from California State University–Monterey Bay. Jessica lives in Henderson, Nevada, with her husband, Chad, and their dog, Gracie. She enjoys traveling, drawing, western history, and photography.